THINK SAFE
ACT SAFE
STAY SAFE

WITH THE
R.E.A.C.T.
APPROACH TO SELF DEFENCE

STEVE COLLINS

HarperCollins*Publishers*

HarperCollins Publishers
Westerhill Rd, Bishopbriggs, Glasgow G64 2QT

www.**fire**and**water**.com

A PS5 book first created by
 PS5 Ltd, Nemus House, London Rd,
 Stockport, Cheshire, SK7 4AH UK

First published 2001

Reprint 10 9 8 7 6 5 4 3 2 1 0

© Steve Collins 2001

ISBN 0 00 710236 4

A catalogue record for this book is available from The British Library

Design & Art Direction by Steve Collins
Photography & Artwork by PS5

Steve Collins asserts his moral right to be identified as the author of this work

Printed in Great Britain by The Bath Press

"The greatest warrior wins without fighting"

Sun Tzu's
Art of War
circa 500BC

ABOUT THE AUTHOR

In the summer of 1956, at just seven years old, Steve was introduced to the gentle art of jujutsu, which marked the beginning of his lifelong love for the martial arts. The profound thoughts and skills of the ancient masters fascinated him from an early age and the study of these ancient combat systems became an interest he is passionate about. Over the years Steve has had the privilege of training with, and under, some of the world's most eminent authorities in martial arts, self-defence and personal protection. He has studied most of the well-known martial arts like judo, jujutsu, karate, aikido, aikijujutsu and hapkido as well as some of the more militaristic close-quarter combat systems used by law enforcement professionals and special forces. He has achieved black belt dan grades in several disciplines and was recently honoured by the International Ki Do Association with a master's degree as a recognised authority and instructor in close-quarter personal protection.

Although Steve's personal career moved in a different direction and he became a professional commercial designer, in 1986 he established his own design consultancy specialising in law enforcement, defence and security. This gave him an ideal opportunity to take advantage of his knowledge in combat skills that he had developed over a period of thirty years. As a civilian working in a very sensitive field he is privileged to see many aspects of close protection, self-defence and officer safety training and, as a result, a great deal of his time spent studying combat systems has centred around the use of weapons and defensive tactics against weapons. Through his work with many security professionals, Steve recognised there was a very real need for training material on the subject of concealable weapons, their use and methods of concealment, and in 1999 wrote *The Manual of Prohibited and Concealable Weapons*, widely considered to be the definitive training aid and in use with government authorities across the globe. It was during the writing of this weapon awareness manual for law enforcement training that Steve began to formulate his ideas for an awareness publication for the general public and the **REACT** system of self-defence was born.

Instances of violence and violent attacks are on the increase. Whoever you are and wherever you are, you are more likely to encounter physical violence today that at any time in the past. Steve has developed **REACT** especially for all those of you who have neither the time nor the inclination to study fighting systems. It is not just another self-defence system weighed down by complicated and sometimes impractical martial arts techniques. **REACT** is for everyone. The system is universal and the principles apply whether you are on the streets of New York, London, Johannesburg or Tokyo. The concept is so versatile that it can be utilised by anyone, no matter what their lifestyle or occupation. Steve maintains that anyone is capable of successfully protecting themselves, regardless of their age, sex, strength or level of physical fitness, and he has specifically designed **REACT** to be easy to remember and simple to follow, which makes the system one of the most exciting concepts in personal protection and self-defence available today.

REACT works. It will work for you. It will work for everybody!

Dedicated to all those people who have successfully defended themselves or others without ever taking a self-defence lesson or reading a book like this. To those who recognised their enemy's weaknesses, were empowered by their own strengths and took control.

You are an inspiration to us all.

ACKNOWLEDGEMENT

I would like to thank all the following people for their help and assistance with the production of **REACT**. All those who suffered the indignities of being punched, kicked, grabbed and groped in the name of self-protection. Special thanks to Mark Goodwin for the many times he burnt the midnight oil with me. Also Dave Stranaghan, for his superb photography. And extra special thanks to Debs, without whom the whole project would probably have never been completed. Her uncanny ability to understand and type from my totally illegible scribbles saved the day on many occasions.

Tony Blauer

My special thanks to Tony for not only having the insight and skill to develop the genetically inspired S.P.E.A.R. SYSTEM™, but also for his recognition of the synergy between it and **REACT**. I am grateful that he agreed to contribute to this book as a way of furthering our joint pursuit of promoting the idea of effective personal protection for everyone.

Tony training special operations team in the USA

Gary Ashton
Alan Barnard
Gunter Bauer
Jonathan Beckett
Sue Beckett
Tony Blauer
Andrea Brady
John Cordingley
Pierre Dalloz
Deborah Duckworth
Linda Fone
Chris George
Roger Gillatt
Ron Gillatt
John Giorgio
Mark Goodwin
Dave Hodgson
John Hughes
Steve Janes
Charlie Jarman
Brian Jenkins
Phil Kay
John Kenyon
Louise Mainwaring
Debbie McConnell
Elaine Musgrave
Geoff Ridgway
Debbie Sowerbutts
Janet Spencer
Dave Stranaghan
Elaine Stranaghan
Vic Thompson
Diane Warren
&
Boris the spider

CONTENTS

R E A C T
INTRODUCTION

In the absence of a utopian society where everybody loves his neighbour, the sun always shines and bluebirds fill the skies, every man, woman and child on the planet needs some way of defending themselves. In fact, we all perform defensive strategies in our daily lives without even being aware of it. The child who walks a different way to school each morning to avoid the class bully is actually implementing a defensive strategy. Putting your seat belt on when you get into your car is a defensive strategy. Flinching and yelling out when startled is also a form of defensive strategy. It is part of our natural instinct to survive.

Most of us have a natural built-in instinct to try and avoid trouble if we possibly can. However, the sad but stark reality is that violent crime has become a worldwide social disease of epidemic proportions. It has been steadily on the increase over the last fifty years. Children are murdered or subjected to horrific cruelty and abuse, old ladies are raped in their sick beds, young women are regularly savaged in public places, men and boys are beaten, stabbed and shot to death on our streets every day. I am not qualified to even attempt to try and explain why this is, or moralise about the state of today's society, but what I can say, without fear of contradiction, is that it will probably get worse before it even starts to get better. Thus, if you accept this you owe it to yourself to learn how to increase your chances of survival. We've all read about the needless suffering of innocent people time and time again and yet, in the majority of cases, with a little knowledge these people could have avoided a violent and dangerous situation. Living in a jungle doesn't mean you should accept the role of prey to the predators that are, without doubt, out there.

How many times have you thought 'it will never happen to me' or 'well, if it's going to happen it's going to happen, there's nothing I can do about it'? Has your religion conditioned you to 'turn the other cheek'? All of these attitudes will get you into deep trouble on the streets. It might just happen to you; in fact, statistics show there is a strong possibility that it will. But if it's going to happen there is something you can do about it. Co-operate with a mugger and you will be mugged, co-operate with a rapist and you will be raped, co-operate with a murderer and you will be murdered, and that 'turn the other cheek' thing means you just get that one punched as well, or worse still, slashed with a knife.

Threat or no threat, what do you think?

Most large cities have seen a rapid decline in people's respect for one another, resulting in aggression, selfishness and a huge number of individuals living in constant fear of attack. Despite this increase in violence most people mistakenly believe that it is the job of the police to protect us from harm. That's where we're wrong – it is the job of the police to enforce and uphold the laws of the country. It is up to us to take steps to ensure our own safety and that of our family. There are people out there who were never endowed with a social conscience; the only pain they acknowledge is their own. The sociopaths are all around us, the problem is that they look just like you and I. They are society's predators and they will always prey on the weak, or what they perceive to be a 'soft' target. The behaviour of these types can range from the manipulator, whose sole purpose is self-gratification at the expense, or even pain of others, to the extreme of the serial killer. Their primary characteristics are that they have no regard for anybody, other than what they can take from them. The sociopath will happily beat their victim to a pulp without feeling one second of remorse or guilt. These predators want your property, your body, your life or all three, and believe it is their right to take any, or all of them.

But let's be positive. You do not have to accept that it's inevitable you will fall prey to these people. Don't adopt a passive stance, although you must accept that you will probably, at some time in your life, come into contact with a situation that may be potentially dangerous. This isn't to say that you should take the law into your own hands, but it does mean that you should take responsibility for your own protection and arm yourself with the knowledge and ability to do so. Very few things happen on the streets that aren't detectable in advance, but if you're not alert and aware you won't see the danger signs.

So what can you do?

Most people automatically think of the martial arts such as judo, jujutsu, karate and aikido, which is fine as far as it goes. I have been involved in the martial arts, in one way or another, since 1956. I am the proud owner of literally hundreds of books on the subject. I have studied, practised and taught the martial arts for most of my life. I have had the privilege of training with some of the world's most eminent masters and authorities and I would like to think I have achieved a reasonably high level of competence. One thing is for sure, I have

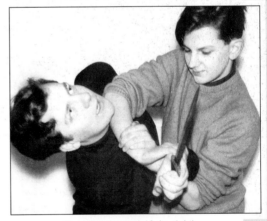
The author aged 12 (to right)

loved every minute of it and wouldn't have missed this experience for the world. However, in truth, out of the thousands of techniques and combinations taught – strikes, kicks, punches, projections, pins, chokes, throws, locks and neutralisations, few are relevant in a real-life street situation.

Being a martial artist does not mean you are able to defend yourself. The techniques a traditional practitioner studies and may even become highly skilled in, can be your worst enemy in a real fight. Two or three instinctive and well-practised moves are all you actually need. Please don't think I am saying martial arts are a waste of time; they are not and a good grounding in them gives you a degree of physical fitness, good reflexes, good balance, good timing and an awareness others don't possess. The main problem is that most of the martial arts are taught and practised as sports, with a small amount of self-defence thrown in for good measure and to make it a bit more interesting. Unfortunately, the self-defence is not usually very realistic and is based on classical and formalised attacks and defence techniques, and so much of the self-defence taught in martial arts schools only works if your training partner allows it to.

A beautifully executed Aikido technique

Remember that martial arts, self-defence and fighting are three very different things. A martial art is just that – an art. Practitioners spend a lifetime practising and perfecting highly complex combat techniques. Even many of today's supremely skilled masters are only masters of modern, watered-down adaptations of the original combat systems developed for the battlefield. These original combat skills were for fighting, while the modern martial arts we know today are designed for study and not for combat. In self-defence the goal is to avoid harm, to survive. In self-defence it should be completely unnecessary to confront and in fact, it is preferable that we don't confront unless it is absolutely unavoidable. Even if physical confrontation becomes inevitable you must extract yourself at the first possible opportunity. For 'extract yourself' read 'run away'. The best place to be when 'the shit hits the fan' is somewhere else! This may not be good for your ego, but we are talking self-defence, self-preservation. Don't endanger yourself and others by fighting just to prove that you can, and don't confuse ego with honour. Honour is your strength of character and your integrity. No-one can take that from you. Your ego, on the other hand, can get you hurt or even killed. You must look on self-defence as a necessity and understand how to minimise the risk of an attack.

The aim of fighting is to defeat an opponent or an enemy. Soldiers fight: it's their job to kill or even be killed if necessary, for their country. A boxer fights, some are paid huge amounts of money to get knocked around the ring and hopefully come out on top. So, unless you are a professional fighter there should never be any need to do it, but if you are faced with having to fight remember that a real fight on the street rarely lasts more than 20 seconds, it is not a game and there are no rules. You must take control.

Trained to kill

So how do we do that? How do we give ourselves the edge that enables us to walk away from a nasty situation, preferably unharmed? You need to be aware that human behaviour, both your own and your assailant's, can't be predicted with any degree of certainty, particularly in a stressful situation, so there's no point in pretending it's easy, or there's some mystical, magic wand that will make it all go away. Don't kid yourself that you will leap into action with fists of fury and vanquish your assailant. You won't. But there are things you can do and they are summed up in one little word – **REACT**.

REACT is not just a clever name thought up by marketing people; it is a system that enables you to stay in tune with your environment, to be relaxed but alert, aware of your surroundings and switched on to any escalation in your personal threat level. **REACT** is a defensive strategy, not a martial art or a method of fighting. In fact you could say it's a system of how to *avoid* fighting and that's exactly my aim in writing this book, to teach you how to avoid conflict and confrontation. If, however, all your preventive efforts fail and you do face an actual attack, I will also show you some simple yet effective techniques and tactics to help you act to your best advantage in the event of a violent attack.

Most of you reading this book will drive a car and many of you will have driven for years and travelled tens of thousands of miles. Every time you get into your vehicle, fasten your seat belt and commence your journey, whether you are aware of it or not, you apply the principles of **REACT**. You are conditioned to recognise that driving from A to B could be potentially dangerous. So what do you do? You switch on, you become more aware, you look ahead, you look behind, you become acutely aware of other vehicles, intersections, side streets, road signs, traffic lights, pedestrian crossings, children. In fact a huge amount of visual and mental stimulus is being processed by you, and all at thirty, forty, fifty miles per hour or more. And why? Because it's instinctive. You do it automatically in order to maintain your progress and arrive at your destination safe and in one piece by avoiding an accident. Why not apply this attitude of mind when you are walking around? At three miles per hour it should be much easier! The **REACT** system helps you to remember, the **REACT** system helps you to switch on to your environment. Think of it as

Switched on to potential danger

your personal tool box with five separate drawers. Each drawer contains all
the tools you need, just choose the appropriate tool to deal with each
situation. All the drawers are clearly labelled to help you to remember
their contents.

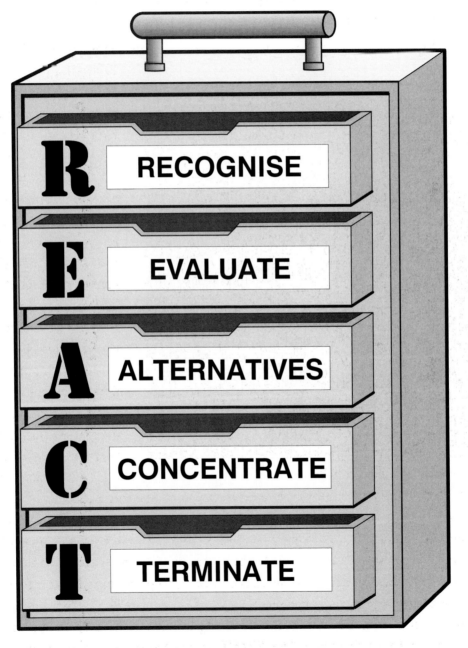

Let's examine the drawers one by one...

REACT ❯

RECOGNISE

Before we can even begin to recognise potential danger we must first accept that the possibility of a threat actually exists. Unfortunately, there will always be a degree of risk in all our lives, not least because we come into contact with many different people in many different places every day. We have to accept that we live in a dangerous world and should be prepared to handle it.

So what does danger look like?

This question has many answers because danger will always mean different things to different people, depending upon their particular circumstances. For example, imagine you are walking down a country lane and a man approaches; as you near him you note that he is watching you somewhat intently. Is he going to ask you the time or directions to the nearest bus stop, or is he going to attempt to rob you at knife-point? If you are an advocate of the old adage 'it will never happen to me' and therefore 'ignorance is bliss', you will not even consider that you could be in danger. But the sad reality is that somebody somewhere, every minute of the day and night is being attacked and this person walking towards you could mean that today it's your turn. If you realise he could be a potential threat, you will experience a sensation of danger and a feeling of fear. Fear is an emotional state and we can use it to help us create positive action. Fear is a natural self-defence mechanism and being frightened is no bad thing because the adrenaline rush we experience can make us

Be aware of people around you when using a public telephone kiosk - you could be a prime target for thieves, muggers and rapists

REACT REMINDER

stronger, more positive in our resolve and 'switched on', ready to deal with a dangerous situation if it arises.

▶▶ **REMEMBER, BEING SWITCHED ON DOESN'T MEAN BEING PARANOID.**

It should make you feel safer, in control and more self-assured.

We are all conscious of our five senses of sight, touch, hearing, smell and taste. However, we also have a sixth sense, that of intuition, which is often referred to as our 'gut feeling'.

▶▶ **BEING AWARE OF A POTENTIAL THREAT IS SIMPLY USING OUR SIXTH SENSE.**

We are all guilty of sometimes ignoring our gut feeling, but more often than not if we feel as though something is wrong it probably is wrong. In over 90 per cent of violent crimes committed against an individual, one of the main contributing factors is that the warning signs that would have been there were either ignored or simply not recognised. It is easier to *stay* out of trouble than it is to *get* out of trouble, and so we want to avoid confrontation wherever possible. The most effective way to do this is to be constantly aware of our environment.

Don't ignore your gut feeling

REACT REMINDER ≫≫ Be wary of approaching a car when the driver appears to be asking for directions

Condition Red !

COOPER'S COLOUR CODES

Jeff Cooper was an American military combat pistol instructor who believed there was a need for an instant way of recognising the escalation of threat levels encountered by his trainees, and developed a colour coding system that he called 'conditions'. Although his system was originally developed over 50 years ago, these colour-coded conditions still work for us today in our everyday environment. These conditions are psychological states of increasing awareness accentuated by visualising the colours white, yellow, orange and red. Let's look at each condition and what it represents.

On a busy street, always carry your bag or briefcase on the side furthest away from the road

REACT
REMINDER

R
E
A
C
T

CONDITION WHITE

This condition is where the majority of people spend the majority of their time. In this state you are completely unaware of your surroundings, looking but not seeing and totally unprepared for even the prospect of danger. Condition White is the victim state and predators will always 'home-in' on people in this vulnerable condition. We are particularly at risk from falling into Condition White when we are in familiar surroundings, it's quiet and our minds are a million miles away – a state familiar to us all.

 THE ONLY TIME IT'S ACCEPTABLE TO BE IN CONDITION WHITE IS WHEN YOU'RE ASLEEP.

CONDITION YELLOW

From the moment you wake up in the morning you should be in Condition Yellow 100 per cent of the time. You should be relaxed but alert, aware of your surroundings and, although you aren't expecting any trouble, you would be able to recognise a problem if one arose. Being in Condition Yellow gives you a presence and transmits a signal that says you are not a victim. Remember, being 'switched on' and aware is not being paranoid but simply moving through your environment in a confident and alert manner.

CONDITION ORANGE

Alarm bells are now ringing! There has been a change in your environment and you are aware that a potential problem has arisen. Your mind is reacting and beginning to evaluate the level of danger and threat you may be faced with.

CONDITION RED

The potential problem has now become a real incident. It is directed at you and you take action and decide how you are going to 'terminate' this situation. The action you take may be simply to extract yourself quickly and quietly, or you may be required to deploy a more physical defensive tactic.

REACT REMINDER >> Try to avoid a set daily routine - unpredictability is more likely to deter a predator

CONDITION

WHITE

THE VICTIM STATE - YOU SHOULD NEVER BE IN THIS CONDITION

CONDITION

YELLOW

'SWITCHED ON' AND ALERT - THIS SHOULD BE YOUR NATURAL STATE

CONDITION

ORANGE

ALARM BELLS - YOU HAVE BECOME AWARE OF A POTENTIAL PROBLEM

CONDITION

RED

ACTION - TERMINATE THE SITUATION NOW

Avoid carrying everything - cheque books, credit cards, keys, identification, cash etc. in one bag

REACT REMINDER

R E A C T

YOUR PERSONAL SPACE

We all have an invisible psychological boundary that surrounds us. This allows us to maintain a protective distance from others. Changes in this distance, especially between you and a potential assailant, will alter both your own and your assailant's perception of a situation, either positively or adversely. You must control your own space.

COMFORT ZONES

Imagine a circle around you at an arm's length in distance. Any person inside this imaginary circle should only be there if you have invited them. If the person inside what we will call your **intimate zone** is a friend or family member, you will be comfortable with the situation. You may even allow them closer in order to have physical contact, such as a hug or kiss. Although this is your intimate zone, and normally reserved for those you trust, remember it is also the zone that you will not only make love in, but also fight in. Of course it is not practical in today's society to maintain this intimate zone exclusively for friends and family. We all invade each other's intimate space every day of our lives, as for example, on a train, in a busy street or at the football stadium where we can be shoulder to shoulder with total strangers. It's not their fault and the circumstances are, to a degree, beyond everyone's control, but these people are inside your intimate zone. Any time anyone is within this distance, whether you know them or not, make sure the distance is appropriate for the situation. Therefore you should be in Condition Orange, switched on to a potential problem. If someone you mistrust is too close to you – move! Shift your position but make sure that you can still see them with your peripheral vision.

▶▶ YOU MUST CONTROL YOUR OWN INTIMATE ZONE.

Being in control of the distance between yourself and others plays a vital role in determining the success or failure of a violent

REACT REMINDER ➤➤ Trust your gut feelings: if you feel that things are somehow not right then they probably aren't and you need to take action

encounter. A thousand miles is a good safe distance to be from trouble, but in the absence of that luxury the next area of space to look at is your **personal zone**. This is the space in which most social interactions take place. Once again, using yourself as the centre of the circle extend the parameters out to about four metres. At first glance this may seem a good, safe distance. You are aware of most things with your peripheral vision and probably feel much more comfortable with people at this distance. Be careful! This is a distance that could easily lull you into a false sense of security. A reasonably mobile and determined aggressor will close that gap and be all over you in less than two seconds, giving you little or no time to respond successfully.

If you stand toe-to-toe with an attacker, you will be hit if he decides to strike. If he is on the edge of your intimate zone, even if you are in Condition Red, the chances are you will still end up with a thick lip. By the time your eye detects a movement and the brain decides on a course of action, it will probably still be too late and so, although you are in a better position to defend yourself, you are in no less danger within your personal zone. If you have recognised the sign of an imminent attack, you must be locked into Condition Red to stand any chance of protecting yourself.

Now we come to our **public zone**, which is from four to approximately twenty metres from your person. Little normal contact takes place at this sort of distance. You are relatively safe from immediate attack (unless your assailant is armed with a gun of course). This is your Condition Yellow space – switched on, alert and perceptive to any person who might just enter your personal or intimate zones uninvited.

Everyone has his/her personal space, even your attacker, and it is important to remember that angry, aggressive and frustrated people need more personal space than normal.

**R
E
A
C
T**

Avoid travelling alone whenever reasonably possible, especially at night

**《 REACT
REMINDER**

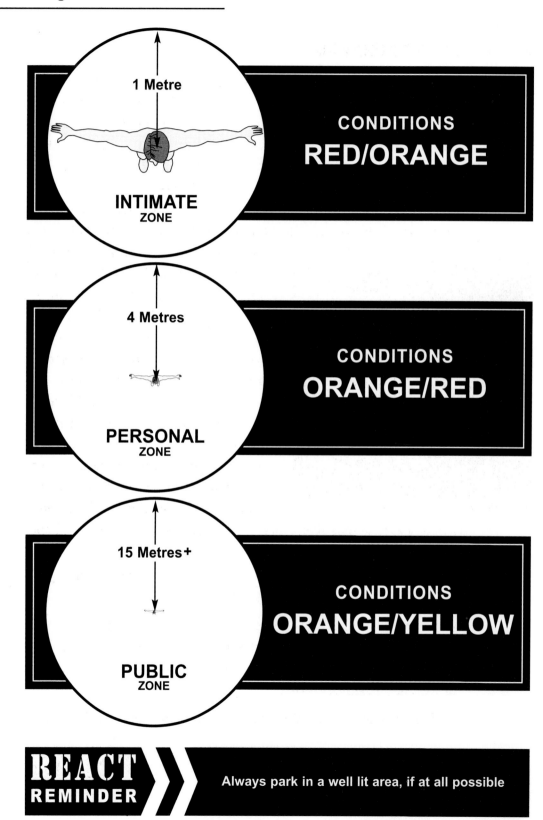

1 Metre

INTIMATE
ZONE

CONDITIONS
RED/ORANGE

4 Metres

PERSONAL
ZONE

CONDITIONS
ORANGE/RED

15 Metres+

PUBLIC
ZONE

CONDITIONS
ORANGE/YELLOW

REACT

REACT
REMINDER 》》 Always park in a well lit area, if at all possible

SITUATION AWARENESS

An awareness of your surroundings and location is the cornerstone of good personal security. As I said before, *it is much easier to stay out of trouble than it is to get out of trouble.* One of the best ways to stay out of trouble is to keep away from the sort of places it is likely to happen. If you are ignorant of your environment and believe 'it will never happen to me', you may as well walk around with a great big neon sign saying 'victim'. We can all think of places in the world where we would not want to be under any circumstances. Bad places

Your safety is your responsibility

exist all over the planet and they tend to look like bad places. For instance, you probably wouldn't choose to go to Bosnia for a holiday at the moment. So why would you still consider walking down a dark and deserted alleyway at night just because it's fairly close to your home? Whether it's round the corner from your house or the back streets of Beirut, these are the places the predator lurks. Remember that sixth sense, that gut feeling, and listen to it. If it looks like a snake, sounds like a snake and smells like a snake it probably is a snake, so stay away from it.

 IT STANDS TO REASON – STAY AWAY FROM BAD THINGS, BAD PLACES AND BAD PEOPLE AND THEY CAN'T HURT YOU.

Situation awareness is recognising potentially dangerous environments, but be aware that some of the most peaceful-looking locations can still be affected by crime. Nowhere should be thought of as being completely safe.

Situation awareness also means recognising safer environments

Don't record a message on your answer-phone that indicates you live alone. If you are female ask a male friend to record the message **REACT** REMINDER

such as good, well-lit parking spots, populated areas with lots of bright lights, the local police station (it's always a good idea to know where you can find the police). A developed sense of awareness will not only help you keep out of trouble, but also give you some options to escape from it.

THREAT AWARENESS

We've just looked at being switched on to your environment, but don't let your location threaten you more than an actual attack. Sure,

Protect your intimate zone

stay away from dark alleyways, but a knife at your throat in a multi-storey car park, a knife at your throat on the riverbank or a knife at your throat in your home is still a knife at your throat. The place makes no difference to the severity of the attack. So, as situation awareness is being aware of your location, threat awareness is being aware of the people in your location. It's the predator with the knife that will hurt you, not the dark alleyway. Therefore, threat awareness is your first line of defence. It is essential

that you know what is going on all around you all the time.

 THREAT AWARENESS IS YOUR EARLY WARNING SYSTEM.

The quicker you become aware of a problem the less likely it is to take you by surprise and it's not good enough just to look – you have to see. Open your eyes and really look at what's happening around you. Ask questions. 'Is that person over there looking at me?' and if so, 'why?' These questions are your defensive strategy. Look, look and look again. Be aware of people's demeanour, facial

REACT REMINDER ›› Never walk down the street close to buildings, especially at night. A potential attacker could drag you into a doorway

R
E
A
C
T

expressions and the way they carry themselves. Be aware of little things people say and learn to read between the lines. A snide comment or the tone in a voice can give away their true intent. Be aware of people's hands, especially if they are within your intimate or personal zones. Look for the little signs. Remember the snake: if it looks and acts like one, it probably is one.

STAYING ALERT

All this talk of being switched on, recognising the potential threat, colour codes, comfort zones, situation and threat awareness is all well and good but how do we do it?

 EASY! TURN IT INTO A GAME THAT YOU PLAY EVERY DAY.

You don't need to walk around a paranoid nervous wreck looking over your shoulder every few seconds. Take on the role of the predator, play 'look for the victim'. Try to spot why they look like a victim, what makes them vulnerable and if you were a villain, how you would approach or even attack them. Spot those people who are in Condition White with those big neon signs saying 'victim'. Look for the people who are switched on and remember that the most switched-on person on the street will be the criminal. See if you can spot a likely culprit. Ask yourself what it is that makes certain people look confident and unapproachable. Turn it into a game – it will help you learn to be your own bodyguard. Also, ask yourself simple questions: Can I afford to be in a fight? Can I afford to lose my money or my belongings? Can I afford to be beaten and spend time in hospital and away from my work? If I were to be killed, how would my family and friends fare without me? Keep these questions in your mind. Have the will to survive, think **REACT** and always remember your safety is your responsibility, you can't always rely on help being at hand. Make staying alert part of your daily life but don't become obsessed, treat it as a game.

Never take shortcuts through empty car parks, deserted parks or unlit areas, especially at night

REACT REMINDER

R
E
A
C
T

REACT ▶

EVALUATE

So you have recognised that there is a potentially nasty situation brewing, which could quite possibly be a threat to your personal safety. But what exactly does that mean? How do you tell if someone is just going to hurt your feelings or try to tear your head off? Evaluating the level of danger is your next step. Of course, your perception of the threat will vary from situation to situation: the more determined and aggressive your antagonist is, the higher the threat level, and of course your response will vary accordingly. A low-level threat can often be resolved with some tactical dialogue which will verbally diffuse the situation. However, high-level threats will require a more positive, dynamic and possibly physical action. High-level threats fall into the category of a survival response where you need to take over the situation and do whatever you deem necessary to terminate the danger. Remember, it is you and only you that can take the initiative and decide on the level of danger you perceive yourself to be in. If you firmly believe you are at serious risk, get challenged, get positive, get aggressive and terminate!

The escalation of a situation, or indeed conversely, its de-escalation, can happen extremely quickly. Of course de-escalation is exactly what you are looking for, extracting yourself from the danger with as little fuss as possible and, hopefully, no physical damage to either you or your antagonist (especially you). But how do you know if it's going to go in the wrong direction? How can you tell if the situation is going to escalate into a bloodbath? Quite often the

R
E
A
C
T

Take care not to put any identification down on a shop or restaurant counter where other people can read your name and address

REACT REMINDER

direction in which the threat level goes is totally within your control. It stands to reason that nobody will attack, or attempt to rob or rape you, if they think you are going to successfully defend yourself. They may not be nice people but they are not totally stupid, and that's why you are in control. It is the assailant's perception of you that determines the direction the situation goes in.

▶▶ VICTIMS LOOK LIKE VICTIMS, EASY TARGETS LOOK LIKE EASY TARGETS.

You do not need to be built like Arnold Schwarzenegger to be able to defend yourself. Size is irrelevant. However, you do need to

You don't need big biceps to protect yourself

cultivate an ability to transmit signals that tell others you are switched on, aware, confident and not to be messed with.

 DO NOT DISPLAY VULNERABILITY TO THE OUTSIDE WORLD.

If you are giving off signals then so are other people and it is those signals that enable you to evaluate a situation. A potential attacker will be reading your body language and their decision to attack you or not will be based largely on their perception of whether or not you are an easy target. Play the role of the victim and you will be victimised. Give off signals that say 'No, I am not

R
E
A
C
T

REACT REMINDER ▷▷ On public transport always sit close to a companion or the driver/conductor. Avoid the seat nearest the exit

a victim,' and a potential assailant will think twice. By saying 'no!' I don't just mean directing it to your attacker – it is more important to say 'no!' to yourself. You must give yourself a directive and permission to take control. I repeat: get challenged, get positive, get aggressive and terminate!

Developing threat awareness is more than just being aware that you may be in danger and accepting that you may need to take steps to protect yourself, and more than spending the rest of your life looking over your shoulder. After reading this book you will be aware that you possess an incredibly powerful psychological and physical arsenal. The key is to develop a focus that enables you not only to know that you have these powers, but to recognise how and when to use them. This means that you need to learn how to evaluate a situation and read the signs. Let's assume you and I are normal, well-balanced, law-abiding citizens. You are out for the evening with your partner at a nice bar. You are enjoying the conversation and the company of your date when a total stranger, quite accidentally, bumps into you and spills your drink. Even though he obviously did

What do you do?

If you are female and live alone, never disclose your title or first name in the telephone book or on your doorplate

REACT
REMINDER

not intend to do this on purpose, it was undoubtedly his fault; however, his response to the accident is not to apologise but to have the audacity to tell you to open your eyes and watch where you're going in a very aggressive manner.

What do you do?

A   *Instantly turn on him, plunge your thumbs into his eyes, simultaneously grabbing his hair and head-butting him, breaking his nose. Snap his head down and drive your knee into his face, fracturing his jaw and smashing his teeth. As he falls to the floor in the foetus position, knee-drop him in the kidneys then finish him off with a series of kicks, dislocating his knee joints and breaking his ankles.*

B   *'Excuse me, friend, but I think that was your fault and you're the one that needs to open your eyes and watch where you're going. I expect an apology and a fresh drink. Someone needs to teach you some manners.'*

C   *'Terribly sorry, I'll try to be more careful in the future.'*

D   *Nothing.*

Which is the right thing to do?

A   Totally out of context and inappropriate to the situation. This person is obviously a clumsy, ignorant buffoon, but he does not deserve to spend six weeks in intensive care. However, you would deserve to spend six months in prison.

B   This is a fantasy. It's straight off a film set. It's what your ego wants you to say, but it would be inappropriate for two reasons. The first is ethical, in that, if by your response this situation now escalates into an ugly fight, it is your fault. This man may be a

REACT

REACT REMINDER ›› Avoid sitting near to the till in a restaurant or bar - these are the most likely places for a robbery

fool but at least he was walking away and you have now challenged his ego. If all you want to do is create an opportunity to show off your fighting skills to your partner, you are a bigger fool than he is. The second reason this response would be wrong is that this person has already shown aggression. Why confront a person who has already displayed an aggressive posture towards you for something that was obviously not your fault in the first place? Your evaluation should tell you that he is probably prepared to resort to violence if pushed and that is an undesirable conclusion to the situation.

C This response could be described as being a bit of a smart arse! We all do it, most of us only think of it after the event but, on the spur of the moment, sometimes we just can't help ourselves. The snappy, pithy, sarcastic retort makes us feel good, but remember it could also get you a black eye.

D Nothing – that's the one. Sorry, it may not be what you want to hear, but nothing is the thing to do. Your evaluation of this situation should be that this person has no regard for other people. He may not have bumped into you on purpose, but he is so arrogant and ignorant that his ego will not allow him to apologise. He would rather be belligerent and aggressive and blame you, rather than lose face. You do not know his circumstances, he may be angry or upset over something totally unrelated and just looking for something or somebody to take his frustrations out on. He may even be carrying a weapon. Doing nothing has terminated this situation. Although your pride may be a little hurt, you will leave the restaurant safe and in one piece. You will also have undoubtedly convinced your date that, if he had tried something, you would have easily wiped the floor with him!

R
E
A
C
T

When getting into a lift, if you feel uncomfortable about your fellow passengers, don't feel embarrassed about getting out and taking the next lift   **《《 REACT REMINDER**

TYPES OF THREAT

It is one thing to have recognised that there is a threat, but it is just as important to identify and understand what type of threat you could be facing. Threats tend to fall into four main categories

INSTANT

This one doesn't need much explanation. It is sudden violence. A surprise attack or ambush. An immediate physical assault on your person. It is obviously the most dangerous because it will happen without warning or apparent reason. Following the **REACT** system should cut down the chances of this type of instant threat, but be aware that shit happens.

INTENDED

You will spot this type of threat early as the assailant tends to give himself away with aggressive dialogue and threatening postures. This combination, more often than not, is the forerunner of an actual physical attack. Drunkeness is usually a major ingredient, because alcohol fuels the aggression of potential attackers. Check your personal space and comfort zone – they are a critical factor when dealing with an intended threat.

UNDUE ATTENTION

A person or group of people are paying you too much attention. Of course it could be quite innocent, but always assume that it is not. If they appear to be talking amongst themselves, but looking at you and perhaps even pointing, you could be being set up for something. If it is a person on their own, they could be weighing you up as a potential victim. Undue attention normally happens on the periphery of your personal zone. Keep them there, but move away to a safer distance and if possible, find the protection of other people.

LOCATION

Don't be threatened by your location. Always remember it's not the

REACT REMINDER >> Use reflections in shop windows, shiny cars and car mirrors to see if you're being followed

place that will get you, it's the people in it. Having said that, we can all find ourselves in undesirable places from time to time. All major cities around the world have areas that you should just stay away from. Of course this is not always possible and people get lost, finding themselves in undesirable places by accident. On the other hand, your work may require you to frequent run-down or semi-derelict neighbourhoods. We all have to use underground or multi-storey car parks on occasions, or sometimes have to visit a high-rise tenement or block of flats. Stairways, corridors and landings can all be potentially dangerous places. Lifts and elevators can be especially dangerous, so check them before you get in and stay alert to the possibility of someone jumping in just before the doors close. Remember, your situation awareness is recognising potentially dangerous environments. Nowhere is totally safe but some locations are obviously worse than others.

WHO IS THE THREAT?

Prevention is better than cure and really that's what **REACT** is all about – using your common sense and a little forward-thinking as you travel through life. It should be relatively easy to stay away from danger and trouble. Spotting trouble, or potential trouble long before it has happened is the master plan. However, crime is a sad fact of life and we can all fall victim to it. Who are these people that prey on society? Unfortunately, less is known about those who commit violent crime than those who are its victims, but it is a fact that they tend to fall into certain demographic profiles. Almost 90 per cent of those arrested for violent crime are males between the ages of 25 and 29, and a disproportionate number are from ethnic and racial minorities. Up to 50 per cent of robberies and assaults are committed by multiple assailants. Street gangs regularly participate in violent crime and muggings. This can be for several reasons such as to maintain the gang's reputation, to protect their

On an escalator, particularly on the underground, keep your handbag nearest to the wall, away from people on the opposite escalator

REACT REMINDER

R
E
A
C
T

territory and to fund alcohol- and drug abuse. Some gangs actually reward members who have the prowess for violence. Many offenders are poorly educated and often have a low IQ. They tend to come from low-income families and are very often influenced by other family members' criminal behaviour. Living in high crime neighbourhoods, in poor housing conditions, with heavy alcohol- or drug abuse can all be major factors in violent and criminal behaviour. Chronic drug and alcohol abuse affect the nervous system and increase the risk of becoming violent. See how we are starting to build a picture of the types of people to stay away from or just keep an eye out for? Of course, this does not mean that you can't be attacked by a twelve-year-old child or a little old lady, although such types of attacker are obviously in the minority.

BECOMING STREETWISE

You have all heard the term 'streetwise', and the most streetwise people out there are the criminals. From your point of view, becoming streetwise is a major ingredient for successful self-defence, and all it actually means is understanding how to function safely in your environment. You need to know the places to stay away from. Where are all the pubs and clubs? Are there drug dealers or gangs in certain areas? Which street corners tend to have hordes of teenage kids hanging around? Do you know where muggings or other violent crimes have occurred in your town? Where are the places to avoid? Some may be just a few yards from where you actually live. Wasteland, canal towpaths, riverbanks, public parks, building sites, dark country lanes. Be aware that being on your own in such places can be dangerous. Start to become streetwise; you are responsible for your own safety so make it your business to find out where you are safe and where you are not.

Let's look at some specifics in a little more detail.

REACT REMINDER ▶▶ If your bag is snatched, don't pursue the thief. They will almost always head for isolated back streets, or the like, to examine the stolen goods

R
E
A
C
T

DRUNKS

Violence often occurs in or just outside bars and clubs at closing time. Tension could have built up over the evening but only erupts when the drinkers get outside. Being in the wrong place at the wrong time is your biggest danger here and getting involved in someone else's dispute is just what you don't want.

Street drunks are not hard to identify, but don't underestimate anyone who is drunk. He may seem like a pushover but remember, the effects of the alcohol can make a person more dangerous: it will have increased his level of aggression and his pain threshold will also be higher. So, do not fight with a drunk. Get out of his way and don't bother to try to reason with him because it's a complete waste of time. Don't maintain eye contact, just try and ignore him. Leave him alone. Keep moving, side-step, turn and walk away. Ignore any ranting and raving. Remember, you are co-ordinated while he is not so getting away should be easy.

JUNKIES

Drug addicts are initially harder to spot. They can have either enlarged pupils or pin-point pupils, depending on the drugs they have taken. At times they will appear to be hyperactive and full of nervous energy. Their speech may be babbling and incoherent, although not in the same way as a drunk slurring his words but trying to sound sober. There is a distinct possibility that the drug addict may be in pain due to withdrawal symptoms. His general health will be poor and he may not have eaten for several days. Even so, the junkie has to feed his habit and is capable of almost anything to get a fix. That means he is capable of extreme violence. Do not fight – be assertive, move away as quickly as you can. He could be extremely strong, but is unlikely to have much stamina. If you were to run away, it is unlikely that you would be pursued.

Never engage in conversation with a complete stranger who approaches you for no apparent reason »» **REACT REMINDER**

REACT

GANGS

The simple rule here is avoid them at all costs – all of them, whether organised gangs, groups of rowdy youths on street corners or gangs of lager-louts coming out of a soccer stadium angry because their team has lost and looking for someone to take it out on. Wherever you are, on your own, with a partner or friends try and avoid getting too close to aggressive-looking groups of people. One thing to consider and keep in mind is that gangs of young women are quite often capable of violence as extreme as gangs of men.

PROSTITUTES

I am not going to moralise about whether the activities of prostitutes, particularly street-walkers, should be legal or not. Prostitution is the oldest profession in the world and many would argue that the service provided is necessary and does no harm. In some parts of the world

A dangerous game

prostitution is closely regulated by the authorities and is considered to be a perfectly normal, respectable and honourable profession. Contrary to popular belief, it is not just a male thing and both sexes use the services of prostitutes, although the majority of clients are men. If you use prostitutes, especially street-walkers, beware. More often than not there is a criminal element behind the work they do. It is very likely that not too far away there is a pimp or boyfriend watching the activities, and it is extremely common for girls to entice a punter or 'john' back to their place where an accomplice can rob, beat them up or even

REACT **REMINDER** ≫ When using a public WC never put your bag on the floor. Also be wary about hanging it on the back of the door

R
E
A
C
T

blackmail them. Often these girls are armed, especially with knives, mainly for self-protection but also as a means of mugging clients. Picture the situation; there you are on the back seat of your car, trousers round your ankles and a razor at your throat or worse. Give her your wallet, say 'thank you very much' and let her go. Think yourself lucky that it was only your wallet and a little pride that you lost. If you use prostitutes, be aware that you could be playing a very dangerous game.

HIRE CARS

Unlicensed taxis and cabs are a major problem in most large cities around the world and it is quite common to see the drivers of these hire cars being arrested at airports. It is easy to fall into their trap: it's late at night, you have missed the last train, you're cold and it's raining. The unlicensed taxi driver is just looking for someone like you. Most of the time he is only trying to earn a living, but his activities are illegal and these drivers are not insured to carry passengers so if you were to have an accident and were injured you would not be able to claim. However, some have a more sinister motive and they are looking for prey, particularly women. Many young girls have thought they were being taken home by a legitimate taxi, only to find they were actually about to experience a nightmare. Male or female, do not get into an unlicensed taxi, especially on your own. Always use a local hire company that you know and trust, keep their telephone number with you and, if possible, get to know their drivers.

BUSES

Late-night buses can also be a problem. To call a taxi is a much better idea, but if you have no choice and a bus is the only option, then these are some points to remember. Try and sit near the driver and never go upstairs if you are on your own. If a bus stops with a group of rowdy youths on board, don't get on. If it's

If you choose to sit near an open window on public transport take care to protect your belongings from a thief reaching in through the window

the last bus and you have no choice, sit near the driver and other passengers (if any).

TRAINS

Trains present all the same problems as a bus but are potentially much more dangerous, especially if they are the type with individual carriages that are not linked with a corridor. If you get it wrong, you can be trapped in a carriage with a real threat for a long time. Do not hesitate to pull the emergency cord if you are convinced you are in real danger with no means of escape. If you are a woman travelling alone, try to choose a carriage where there are several other passengers, especially other women. Do not get into an empty carriage if you can possibly help it. Be switched on to your fellow passengers. If someone does attempt to interfere with you, protest as loudly as you can and make sure other passengers hear your protests. Trains and train stations around the world seem to attract muggers, rapists, pickpockets and other scum just looking for victims. Be aware.

IN YOUR CAR

Just because you are in your own car, don't be lulled into a false sense of security. There are still things you should do that will increase your personal safety. Obviously, your vehicle should always be in a fully serviceable and reliable condition. Your petrol tank should never be less than half full, so get into the habit of filling the tank as soon as it gets to the halfway mark then you will never run out of petrol. If you are going on a long journey, plan ahead; don't run the risk of getting lost in a bad area. If you do get lost, it is best to ask directions at a shop or petrol station, or better still a police station. Keep your doors locked at all times, especially if you ask directions from a stranger on the road. Do not open any of your doors and only open a window a couple of inches, just enough for you to be able to hear each other. I repeat, keep your doors

REACT REMINDER >> Have your bus or train fare ready in your hand to avoid having to open your bag and display its °contents to other people

locked at all times. It is the first thing you should do when you get into your car. A favourite ploy of muggers and rapists is to jump into cars as they stop or slow down at traffic lights. Do not leave your belongings, handbags, briefcases, mobile phones, etc. on the passenger seat because a thief can be in and away before you can say 'bastard!' Never get yourself blocked in at traffic lights or road junctions, always leave enough space between you and the car in front to be able to manoeuvre around it without having to reverse. A good rule of thumb is to be able to see approximately two feet of road between the end of your bonnet and the bottom of the tyres of the car in front. If you

A sensible reactionary gap

break down, stay in your car and phone the emergency services. If you haven't got a mobile phone, get one and keep it with you all the time.

Turn on your hazard lights, and at night the interior lights, to make the vehicle more visible. It is sometimes considered dangerous to stay in your car if you are on a motorway or highway, therefore stand on the hard shoulder or the grass embankment. If you are a woman and a car stops to offer assistance and the driver or occupants of the vehicle are male, get back into your vehicle, lock the doors and decline the offer politely. Only accept help from the official emergency services.

Choose carefully where you park especially if you know that it will be dark when you return to your vehicle. Avoid multi-storey car

If you think you are being followed in your car, never drive home - go to a populated place such as a petrol station

》 REACT REMINDER

R
E
A
C
T

parks if you can, particularly at night. Don't leave things on display in the vehicle that announce 'a woman's car', e.g. umbrellas on the back seat, kiddies toys, shopping bags, hairbrushes on the parcel shelf, cuddly toys on the back window ledge. You may as well stick a sign in the window that says 'woman on her own, will be back later'. Never park nose in first, always reverse into a parking space because if you do have to run to your car and make a quick getaway, it is much easier, not to mention, safer.

Don't stop

Never stop for hitch-hikers or anybody flagging you down at the side of the road, unless it is the police and even then always insist on seeing a warrant card before getting out of your vehicle. If it looks like a genuine situation or accident, drive on to a safe distance and call the police or other emergency services or report it just as soon as you are able. Being in your own vehicle does give you a greater level of personal protection than if you were out walking for instance, but only if you stay in it.

Road rage is supposed to be a new phenomenon, but I'm not so sure. Just look at old turn-of-the-century movie footage of cities like New York or London with hundreds of horse-drawn vehicles and motor cars literally nose to tail. I can't help thinking there must have been a few frayed tempers even back then. Seeing two drivers exchanging aggressive gestures or gesticulating to each other must have always been a common sight. However, such a confrontation is no different from any other self-defence situation, with one subtle difference – *this time it just might have been your fault.* We all do stupid things from time to time when we are driving. If you have cut someone up, or overtaken in an erratic fashion, or pulled out on someone without looking and the next thing you are aware of are

R
E
A
C
T

REACT
REMINDER >>

Never hitch-hike and never pick up hitch-hikers.
Hitch-hiking is illegal in most countries

flashing lights, a blaring horn and a red-faced individual shaking their fists at you in your rear view mirror, what do you do? Give him the finger? NO! Acknowledge your mistake, say sorry, show no aggression, put your hand to your forehead and shake your head. The worst thing you can do is ignore it and try to make a quick getaway. Just say sorry. Do not unlock the doors, do not get out of the vehicle and do not open the windows, and whatever you do don't smile or try to laugh it off. If you have really pissed someone off, don't make them think that you think it's funny. Look sheepish, diffuse the situation with a non-aggressive mime. Furthermore, if the shoe is on the other foot and you are the one that has been cut-up, although it's not easy, let it go. Life is too short even if you are right and he's wrong! Don't become a victim of road rage.

WALKING AND JOGGING

Walking to work, walking to school, a leisurely stroll or jog in the park, a walk in the countryside. Some of you will love it and some of you will hate it and only walk when you absolutely have to. One thing is for certain, you will at some time or another find yourself on your own, walking somewhere.

Walking alone is generally more dangerous for a woman than a man, but remember that men on their own are regularly attacked and mugged. Also, don't assume that you are safe in the daylight – almost 50 per cent of all assaults happen during the day. When out walking for whatever reason, recreation or necessity, you must think of your comfort zones. Remember that imaginary circle around you – your intimate zone, your personal zone and your public zone. People will be moving in and out of these zones all the time, be switched on to them and more to the point, look as if you are switched on. Send out that message 'Don't mess with me!' Remember our game of looking for the victim, those people with a neon sign saying 'easy prey', and make sure you've left your sign at home!

Walk briskly and confidently - dawdling gives thieves more opportunity to attack   **》REACT REMINDER**

R E A C T

If you do like walking, try and familiarise yourself with the areas you walk in and think about what you would do if you did feel threatened or were accosted. Could you escape if you had to? Are there houses or shops nearby that you could run to? Heavily wooded or very isolated areas may be some of the most beautiful places to walk in, but they can be some of the most potentially dangerous. Evaluate both the place and the people in it, and just because you can't see any other people, don't assume there aren't any.

Body language is your major deterrent. Do not display signs of vulnerability. Walk briskly with a sense of purpose. This is crucial

Recognise and Evaluate

particularly when walking in a city – never look lost or indecisive. The majority of street crime is opportunistic. The criminal lays in wait, sees his prey walking along, not a care in the world with their head in the clouds and totally switched off, with that big neon sign flashing. The opportunity presents itself, the impulse is too great, he can't stop himself, it's just too easy! BANG...and it's all over. Like taking candy from a baby and it's all your fault. Yes, it is! As I keep on saying, an attacker wouldn't even have attempted to attack you if he thought for one second you were going to successfully defend yourself. They may be scum, but they're not stupid and if you are unprepared, you will not

be able to defend yourself. If you are prepared, you will. Of course, there is always the psychopath – the person that just wants to hurt or abuse somebody, anybody, with an overwhelming desire to cause suffering or gain some sexual gratification out of other's pain. Unfortunately, this type tend to be a bit more cunning than the

REACT REMINDER If you're walking or jogging and you suspect you're being stalked in a car, think about running back the way you came - it will be harder for the vehicle to turn around quickly

average street thug, but fortunately a lot rarer. They look just like you or me. They are the person next door and you wouldn't give them a second glance in the street or on that country lane. That is just the point! Give everyone a second look – rule of thumb! Don't trust any strangers. They may be as innocent as the day is long, but why take a chance? Healthy caution is no bad thing. You don't need to be paranoid, but you do need to be switched on.

Anyone can be a victim of crime when out walking. Muggings can happen in a few seconds! Street thugs often operate in teams, one distracting the victim's attention from the front, another gang member attacking from behind – striking or snatching a bag. It's a sad fact that we are never going to stop it happening, but you can try and stop it happening to you. In the Alternatives section of this book *(page 70)* I talk about weapons at hand and I advocate that you do not carry anything that was designed as a weapon, because this can get you into trouble with the law. However, there are many things you can justify having in your possession. For example, when walking in the city you could legitimately have your car keys or an umbrella in your hand and whilst on a quiet country stroll, who's to say you shouldn't be carrying a stout walking stick? Think ahead and evaluate the situations as they unfold in front of you.

How many times have you been walking down the street and a car has pulled up at the side of the road, the window is wound down and someone shouts out: 'Excuse me, can you tell me the way to such and such?' What do you do? Don't tell me, you walk up to the car, bend down and almost stick your head inside the window to look at a map or an address on a scrap of paper. Of course, ninety-nine times out of a hundred, it will be a perfectly innocent and legitimate request, but don't take anything at face value. Stay away from the car. Give directions by all means, but don't get drawn in – why take a chance? Recognise that there could be a potential threat and act accordingly.

R
E
A
C
T

If you wear headphones in a public place you will be less aware of your environment because you cannot hear things going on around you

REACT
REMINDER

AT HOME

This is not a book on home security, so I'm not going to drone on about keeping your doors and windows locked and always putting the door chain on before you open it. You should be doing all those things as a matter of course because otherwise you are just inviting crime.

The principles of **REACT** still apply. Recognise the fact that there are people out there who will enter your home and take your belongings. The consequences of that happening to you are obviously not acceptable, and if the alternatives to prevent it happening are to sit at home 24 hours a day with a loaded shotgun or fit some good home security, then fit the locks, the lights and the bars. The vast majority of crimes against property are committed by unprofessional, adolescent male opportunists, and just as with the mugger, they prefer a soft target. You should seek professional advice on home security systems. Your local police can advise you and recommend a reputable company.

When I talk about home security I mean your personal safety when you are at home. For instance, when answering the door try and identify the caller before you open it. Something as simple as a peep hole can do the trick. If you don't know the person, don't open the door without some sort of door limiter such as a chain or bar in place. Think and evaluate. Don't be mislead by appearances. Always ask to see some sort of identification before you allow anybody into your home.

Check the identification thoroughly and if necessary telephone the caller's organisation to verify their identity. Be suspicious of strangers in an alleged emergency looking for assistance, especially at night. Don't let them in to use the phone; you make the call for them and if you are on your own, never let them know that. If your home is alarmed, make sure you have panic buttons fitted in

REACT

R
E
A
C
T

REACT REMINDER >> When you answer the door or phone, don't let your caller know that you live alone, talk to an imaginary companion to give the impression of others being with you

strategic places, particularly by the door and in your bedroom.

When answering the telephone, if the caller is a stranger, never reveal any details about yourself or your situation. If the caller professes to have the wrong number, ask them to repeat the number they want. Do not give them your number. Even though they have called you they may have dialled randomly, so I repeat – never give any information about yourself, name, address, etc.

Always have a mobile phone in your bedroom at night, and so

if you think you have an intruder in your home, be very quiet, lock the bedroom door if possible and telephone the police. Do not go downstairs to investigate. You don't know how many intruders are there or even if they are armed. As with all self-defence you can only decide how best to handle the situation on the day. However, if you do decide to take a more active line, still lock the door and make that call, but make as much noise as you can, switch on the lights and even if you are alone, call out to an imaginary partner. Most burglars are opportunists and generally don't want a confrontation any more than you do. They will usually flee at the first sign that they have been detected.

R
E
A
C
T

If you suspect your home may have been burgled don't go in to check. Call the police immediately  **REACT REMINDER**

RECOGNISING THE SIGNS

Cultivating a knowledge of body language is a crucial element when evaluating a situation. In the first instance both the attacker and the potential victim will display a certain body language. Remember, victims look like victims and, as I keep saying, an attacker will not come near you if he thinks you might just defend yourself and beat him. He wants something from you, but the last thing he's expecting is pain or to be hurt. Bullies, muggers and rapists depend on their body language to intimidate their victims. If you display a timid and fearful disposition, the predator will identify you as an easy target.

Often, a predator's body language will have an arrogance – a puffed-up chest, a swaggering walk. He will try to make his shoulders look broader and be tensing his muscles. The signs will be there, as clear in their own way as the victim's are. Watch out for the signals and avoid the people who display them.

THE WARNING SIGNS

These are the signs that tell you an attack is possible but not necessarily imminent. The person who blusters and threatens usually doesn't want to go through with an actual attack. However, the warning signs should not be ignored as they can quickly change into danger signs.

- *A red or flushed face can imply that a person isn't really ready to fight or attack although he may want to tear your head off.*

- *Use of foul language. Shouting with belligerent and aggressive dialogue. What do they say about sticks and stones?*

- *Throwing the head and shoulders back and puffing out the chest is the classic way of intimidating your prey by making yourself appear bigger than you really are.*

- *Breathing becoming fast and shallow can cause the aggressor to start to hyperventilate, which is a sure sign of indecisiveness.*

REACT REMINDER >> Most muggings take place between 4 and 6 p.m. when people are finishing work, are tired and not particularly alert

R
E
A
C
T

- *Shaking of fists and lots of exaggerated movements, such as pacing backwards and forwards or kicking the ground, are all gestures designed to make you back down.*

- *Increasing levels of aggression, becoming more irrational, agitated and volatile are all signs of losing control. Watch closely, stay calm and in control.*

Don't take these signs too lightly. You are in a potentially dangerous situation. Even though the body language is that of an outwardly violent person, the signs are all saying 'I don't really want to fight, I just want to frighten you. I want you to give in to me because I look big and I'm loud and scary.'

THE DANGER SIGNS

The aggressor to really watch is the one who displays the danger signs. This person has detached himself and will not see you as another person. He will just see you as a victim and won't hesitate to hurt you or even kill you to get what he wants. These are the danger signs to look out for:

- *The facial colour pales and the face turns ashen white as the blood drains into the main muscle groups in readiness for violent action.*

- *A tight, deliberate voice with white lips which tighten over the teeth.*

- *He bows his head down and the eyes become hooded by the eyebrows resulting in a piercing frown. He looks through you, turning you into an object rather than a person.*

- *His body weight drops and shifts forward into a stance with one foot in front of the other. The shoulders also drop or shift in readiness for the initial strike.*

- *All dialogue exchanges will drop immediately prior to an attack. If all movement ceases and from frantic activity there is suddenly silence and stillness be aware - this is the calm before the storm.*

R
E
A
C
T

Avoid eye-to-eye contact with any stranger who
appears to be 'looking for trouble'

REACT
REMINDER

- *Watch for fist clenching – this lubricates the joints ready for the fight*

- *Hiding or averting the face is often a sign that a person is about to lose control and attack. Looking around and appearing to ignore you is a sure sign of impending violence.*

- *A target glance, a flicker of the eyes towards their preferred target can indicate an imminent entry into your intimate zone.*

So these are the main danger signs. Some of them are obvious while others are quite subtle, but they are all there for you to pick up on and enable you to evaluate the level of danger you could be in. People can and will lie to you but their body language will often give them away.

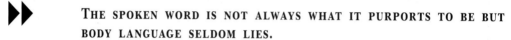 **THE SPOKEN WORD IS NOT ALWAYS WHAT IT PURPORTS TO BE BUT BODY LANGUAGE SELDOM LIES.**

If faced with someone exhibiting typical warning signs, it may be possible to talk your way around the problem. Try to calm him down and diffuse the situation. However, if you are faced with the danger signs your fight or flight options take over and you are in survival mode. You may even have to resort to pre-emptive action.

VERBAL ASSAULT

A verbal assault can be extremely distressing, particularly for a woman. It is common to be attacked verbally well before any physical assault occurs. A tirade of sexually explicit, foul language can take you off guard. If you become the victim of a verbal assault, you have two choices: walk away and ignore it, but be ready should it turn physical; or call his bluff – face him, make resolute eye contact and say something like 'Who do you think you are talking to? How dare you speak to me in that manner!' If there are other people about, make sure they hear you; your voice must be assertive but don't show aggression. Don't wave your arms about, make all your movements slow, precise and focused. Maintain eye contact. Do not allow him

REACT REMINDER If possible don't carry your wages home on pay day - some muggers target their victims on these days particularly

into your intimate zone and do not enter his.

Verbal abuse is sometimes a test whether you'll be provoked into some kind of action, or you back off and submit to his demands. In responding you must use direct commands: 'Keep your mouth shut', 'Don't even think of it', 'Stay away from me'. Stay in control but be aware of the difference between assertiveness and aggression. Keep the tone of your voice down as low as you can, try to control the situation with the power of your assertiveness and avoid any physical contact. If you are a woman you may have the urge to slap him across the face. Resist it! Rest assured that is probably what he wants – you slap him and he beats the crap out of you! Be resolute and strong. You may feel like a jelly inside but don't let him know that. Stay focused and if you have to bluff your way through, remember – your mind is a weapon!

PHYSICAL ASSAULT

Verbal assaults may hurt your feelings but physical assaults just hurt. We have already established that, after reading this book, you will never, under any circumstances, become somebody's victim. But reading this book will not make you invincible (if it did it would have cost you a lot more money!). When evaluating the possibility of an actual physical attack on your person there are certain criteria you must take into consideration. Your attacker – just how big is this guy? If he's 250lbs of ugly meanness who hates everyone in the world, especially you, run away! If your evaluation is such that you don't think this is a person you can reason with and you certainly don't even want to try and fight then get the hell out of there. Extracting yourself is not being a victim, it is terminating the situation to suit you.

REACT is a system of personal protection based on recognition and evaluation of a potential problem. If it is so obvious that someone is about to cause you serious damage, you don't have to be

R

E

A

C

T

If you are attacked, remember your voice is a very effective alarm. Yell and shout to draw attention to yourself, if you can

《 REACT
REMINDER

a brain surgeon to recognise the signs. Violent confrontations and unprovoked attacks are all around us and any one of us can find ourselves in a nasty situation. Physical attacks do happen and we have already looked at the warning and danger signs. Now let's look a little closer. Many martial arts teach you to look into your opponent's eyes. The eyes are the windows to the soul and they say that if you look into your attacker's eyes you will always know his intent.

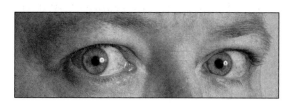

Garbage! If you are looking into your opponent's eyes, you won't see the knife he has just taken out of his pocket. Eyes can't hurt you, hands, feet, guns and knives can and will. Watch the hands! Focus around the height of your opponent's elbows – these are your first indicator that the hands are about to attack. The elbow moves before the hand and moves much more slowly. If the elbow lifts, a hook or circular attack is about to be launched. If the elbow moves forward, it can only be a linear attack, and if the elbow drops back, an attack from the opposite hand is on its way. Try it, go and stand in front of the mirror. Don't stare at the elbow, watch the hands and the elbows with your peripheral vision. Your peripheral vision is better at detecting small movements. For example, how many times have you been sitting at home watching the TV, totally absorbed in your favourite programme, but something catches your attention on the other side of the room? You automatically turn your head to look in the direction of the movement and see a tiny little spider scurrying across the carpet. Your peripheral vision is much more sensitive than your direct vision, therefore, when facing an opponent you should look slightly off-centre of his lead hand and elbow.

The same principle applies to kicks. Watch the knees. Your peripheral vision will pick up on movement you would never see if you were looking into his eyes. Assessing your opponent's movements

REACT REMINDER 〉〉 Never carry your wallet in an 'exposed' back pocket

R
E
A
C
T

is crucial. Evaluate his actions, read the body language, then you should know what he is going to do before he has decided. This isn't magic, it's just common sense.

TYPES OF ATTACK

Consider the different ways a person can actually launch an attack against you. How many can you think of? Your first thought will probably be that there must be hundreds. If you genuinely believe that to be true, try a little exercise. Write a list of all the types of attack you can think of, or think of it in terms of if you were going to attack somebody how many ways you could do it. Don't go off on an ego trip or into the realms of fantasy. Yes, you could shoot somebody from 100 yards away with a high-powered rifle and yes, you could throw a net over someone and drop out of a tree onto them, but it's not very likely. In order to attack somebody you have to enter their intimate zone, so in how many ways do you think you could get that close to another person? I guarantee that you will struggle to write a list that contains more than a dozen or so practical ways to attack and more than likely, less than half a dozen of those would be really effective. Therefore, if there are only really a handful of ways of attacking and only a few of them are primary, you don't need to worry about learning hundreds of different defensive techniques to overcome hundreds of different attacks which won't happen. Regardless of the number of possible attacks there may or may not be, one thing is for sure – your attacker must enter your intimate zone through a window of opportunity and there are four windows.

Imagine your body split into four sections or windows; think of a vertical line from the top of your head down to your toes and a horizontal line at your navel, so the four windows are 'upper left', 'upper right', 'lower left' and 'lower right'. It is unlikely that an attacker will try and attack through two windows at the same

Be aware that standing at a urinal in a men's WC with your back to the rest of the room leaves you in a very vulnerable position 》》 **REACT REMINDER**

R E A C T

time, so if we agree that there are only a handful of really practical ways in which you can be attacked, and there are only four windows of opportunity for an attacker to come through, just how much do you need to know about actual self-defence techniques? The answer is not very much! Judge which window he is going to try and enter and fill the gap with your hands. You don't need to learn fancy blocks and counters. Fill the window and

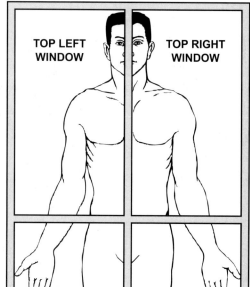

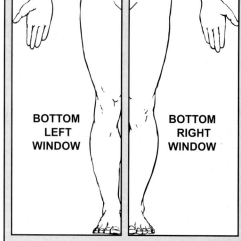

TOP LEFT WINDOW

TOP RIGHT WINDOW

BOTTOM LEFT WINDOW

BOTTOM RIGHT WINDOW

Windows of opportunity

R E A C T

REACT REMINDER ›› Remember, taking action to avoid a conflict isn't cowardice, it's just common sense

drive him back out. If you do have to defend yourself, you don't need to decide exactly what attack is to be launched and then think of the best technique to use to counter it. You don't even need to know how he is going to attack if you know which window he is going to try and come through. It's simple – fill it or move it. If you fill it he will only hit your hands and if you move it you won't be there for him to hit anything.

PRIMARY ATTACKS

Haymaker or punch

Head-butt

Push or grab

Tackle

Head-lock

Kick

 DON'T BOG YOURSELF DOWN WHEN EVALUATING A POSSIBLE ATTACK, REMEMBER THERE'S ONLY A FEW PRACTICAL POSSIBILITIES.

The element of surprise cannot be overemphasised - doing something your attacker least expects can momentarily disarm him

REACT REMINDER

STREET WEAPONS

Your evaluation of any threat will be greatly influenced by whether a weapon of any description has been brought into play, or even whether

you think that your antagonist could be armed. The first thing to remember is your own safety. It is imperative that your only concern is to get away, hopefully uninjured. It is not important that you win or even try to win the fight. If you believe your life to be in danger and there is an opportunity to escape, take it! Run as fast as your legs will carry you! Your flight option should be your first option. However, if escape is impossible, you must comply with your attacker's demands, but only up to the point where you are able to effect an escape or launch your own attack.

Virtually anything can, and has been used as a weapon. In my book *The Manual of Prohibited and Concealable Weapons*, I categorise and give detailed descriptions of over 500 concealable weapons. However, for the purposes of **REACT** we can say that weapons and weapon attacks fall into three categories. That is to say, an attacker is probably going to try and do one of three things:

Shoot something at you.

Stick something in you.

Hit you with something.

Gun, knife, cosh, knuckle-duster, screwdriver, big stick or half a brick, whatever the weapon they all have one thing in common – they can really, really hurt you. But none of them do it on their own. It's not the weapon that attacks you, it's the person holding it. A gun or a knife will not injure you of their own volition, they are inanimate objects. So, do not be intimidated by the weapon, evaluate the person, not what they are holding.

REACT
REMINDER ≫ In an attack your best chance for escape is within the first few seconds

REACT ❯

ALTERNATIVES

Okay, there's a problem and, to the best of your ability, you have evaluated the risk as being of a certain type and level. Your next step is to decide exactly what you are going to do about it. In some ways this is the most difficult section of the **REACT** system to get to grips with.

What are you going to do?

No-one can tell you, I can't even begin to try. Every situation will be totally different and peculiar to your circumstances so every option you have open to you will be different. One thing is for sure, you have to do something and do it now! Is it time to run away? Is it time to fight or is to time to do some quick talking? Whatever your decision is, remember it will be down to you, and only you, on the day. There is, however, one golden rule: you must not telegraph your intentions. Now that is much easier said than done but you must try not to give the game away too soon.

 YOUR ATTACKER SHOULD BE THE LAST ONE TO SEE YOUR DEFENSIVE TACTICS.

Not telegraphing your intentions isn't easy. Think of the various ways we do reveal ourselves without meaning to and make a conscious effort not to do it. Showing anger and losing your temper, adopting an aggressive stance or posture, making verbal threats and threatening gestures, allowing your ego to speak for you – all these will alert your assailant and prepare him to respond. Don't forget

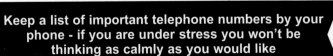 Keep a list of important telephone numbers by your phone - if you are under stress you won't be thinking as calmly as you would like

 **REACT** REMINDER

REACT

R

E

A

C

T

the most obvious one of all, telling your assailant exactly what you intend to do: 'I must warn you that I have studied the **REACT** system of self-defence and if you come any closer I will terminate you.'

A bit of a giveaway   *A non-aggressive posture*

There is a tendency to believe that warnings such as this will deter an attacker. In fact, the reality is they often invite an attack. The only time an attacker should know your intentions is when it is too late for him to do anything about it. Don't give him an opportunity to prepare. Any hint of you being ready to fight will alert him, so however you are standing, leaning, sitting or lying, remain in that position. This is the posture you will fight from. Apart from the fact that you do not have time to reposition yourself into a fighting posture, attempting to do so will warn him of your intentions.

▶▶ YOUR EVERYDAY POSTURE IS YOUR FIGHTING STANCE.

REACT REMINDER ⟫⟫ Men should remember that many women are nervous when on their own. Try not to walk too close behind a woman at night or in an isolated spot

So if you have now decided that you have to do something, and whatever that is you are going to keep it to yourself until you are ready to explode into action, just exactly what options do you have available? As I have already said every situation will always be different and therefore always require a different response. Let's look at the three main alternatives you have available. I will take them in order of my preference, that is to say, the way I think we should want it to happen.

TALK

If you can, try to talk your way out of a situation, but bear in mind that one of the quickest ways to get into a fight is to be drawn into a verbal confrontation. So when I say talk your way out I don't mean argue your way out! Don't give what could be considered as smart-arse or sarcastic retorts. For example, 'What are you looking at?' 'You, and what are you going to do about it?' Don't get drawn in, don't rise to

Try a verbal diffuse

the bait but just say 'Sorry' or 'Excuse me, my mistake'. An aggressive response will more often than not escalate into a violent situation. Although it may go against the grain, don't be reluctant to say sorry. Say it with a smile, be friendly. If you demonstrate non-aggressive intentions they may back off and leave you alone. If not, and the verbal abuse continues, you know that they have seriously underestimated your ability and their over-confidence actually gives

Don't humiliate or argue with someone who is angry or aggravated

REACT REMINDER

R
E
A
C
T

you the edge if the situation starts to escalate in the wrong direction. Hopefully, by responding in a placid manner the tension will be diffused and prove that you have no violent intent whatsoever. If your placid manner, on the other hand, is actually agitating the aggressor, it is often possible to reduce the animosity by the use of empathy. Actually feeling any empathy towards the person is totally irrelevant, just make him feel that you are on his side and if you were him you would be angry too!

▶▶ A FEW CAREFULLY CHOSEN WORDS CAN MAKE ALL THE DIFFERENCE.

Humour is another way of introducing some relief into a tense situation, but once again be careful not to make it sound like you are making fun or laughing at him. Your aim is to get him to lighten up. If he thinks for one second you are 'taking the piss', your humour will have the adverse effect. Friendly dialogue and humour often work, but if for some reason they don't seem appropriate, or more to the point are not working, words can still come to the rescue. Just keep in mind that this type of person is not generally very intelligent but probably extremely streetwise so will pick up on being talked down to or berated. Another ploy is to try and appeal to the lowest common denominator – him! As I have said before, he does not recognise anyone's pain or discomfort other than his own. Ask him how he would feel in this situation. Would he find it acceptable for you to speak to his mother the way he is speaking to you? But choose your words carefully. Don't make him feel as if he has to defend his ego, which he will confuse with his honour. Put him into a position where he can actually back down without losing face. 'OK, piss off, I'll let you off this time.' Phrases like that should be music to your ears. Say thank you politely and walk away. If you have decided that the best way to terminate a situation is with words, you should appear to be non-threatening, as if almost incapable of fighting back. A torrent of aggressive and belligerent expletives will not work, especially on drunks or anyone whose rational thinking has been affected by drugs. Indeed,

REACT REMINDER ⟩⟩ Don't give your telephone number, name and address to strangers for any reason

if your aggressor is so enraged, he won't be able to think straight even if he tried. Be mild mannered. Be his friend. Empathise with him. Use your dialogue to diffuse the situation: 'Hey, what's the problem? I don't want any trouble with you, you seem like a nice guy.'

Confrontations can often be avoided by trying to play on your attacker's emotions. Engage him in conversation, bore him to death with talk of your problems, tell him how you are suicidal because your husband/wife has run away with your neighbour, or you are trying to get to hospital because your mother has just been rushed in with a suspected heart attack. Lie through your teeth. The means justifies the end.

▶▶ **DO NOT, UNDER ANY CIRCUMSTANCES WHATSOEVER, BEG!**

Don't grovel or plead for mercy, this will only serve to give your assailant more power and he will show more aggression towards you. The more you beg, the more he will want to hurt you. The point is to try and make him see you as another person, just like him, and not just another victim. If you can, make him think about his family, his friends or people he feels protective towards. Getting your assailant to think about something else, something that will make him feel emotional towards you, will help you steer him away from wanting to hurt you.

If you can get a person talking to you, and if you can diffuse the situation, there is a distinct possibility that the person can be persuaded to desist and leave you alone. However, if you are not convinced that you are getting it right and you still feel in danger, use dialogue as a distraction. Occupy his mind. Ask him a question. Anything to make him stop and think. Something totally unrelated to the dialogue so far, 'What sort of car do you drive?' or 'Those shoes are nice, where did you get them from?' He will stop, think and then say 'What?' Everybody does, it is a natural reaction. Your train of thought stops for a few seconds as your brain tries to analyse

Don't try to be a hero. Never argue with a robber - you will only anger them and remember that your property is worthless compared to your life **REACT** REMINDER

why you have been asked the question in the first place, and then tries to answer it. In that time you can launch your pre-emptive strike or start to run away.

FLIGHT

Or should we say, run like hell! Get out of there as fast as you can. Flee, extract yourself, call it what you will, but don't look back just go, and go now! If, after all the talk you are still convinced that this

Hit and run

person means to do you serious harm, then don't be a hero. Remember, they can't hurt you if you're no longer there.

Think of some of the skills or knowledge you may already possess. The majority of us have, at some time or another, played or been involved in, or at the very least, watched a sport. If so, you are already aware of the types of moves you need to consider. Obviously, an ability to run is important, but just as important is a capacity to side-step, move backwards, jump, duck, dodge or turn on your heels. We have all done these things, if not last week then certainly when we were kids and you see sportsmen and athletes do them every day.

To say run away is all well and good, but you may need to create a path for yourself. For instance, if there is a wall behind you it could be necessary to power forward and push your aggressor out of the way, or even strike him and side-step or duck under his arm

**R
E
A
C
T**

REACT REMINDER >> Consider your shoes when out for the evening. Can you stamp or kick effectively with them? Be prepared to kick them off if necessary before you are able to run. If he has a wall behind him you may have to jump backwards or spin round in order to escape. As I have said before, only you will know on the day and each situation will be different. Hopefully, it will not be necessary to make any physical contact with your attacker in order to escape.

REMEMBER, AVOIDING CONFLICT IS THE GOAL.

If you do have to strike and run, your strike must be effective. This is not a fight. This is hit-and-run. If your strike is not effective, it will only serve to aggravate your attacker and he will surely come after you. If you have elected to use your flight option, endeavour to effect your escape in a non-violent way. Duck, weave, side-step and then sprint just as if you had come out of the starting blocks at the Olympic Games. A person running is much more difficult to control and attack than a stationary one. This is an important psychological fact to remember. If you are running for your life, you are a force to be reckoned with. The adrenaline is pumping around your body and you are strong. If you have the will to escape, you will find the stamina to keep going.

Don't look back, be completely focused on where you are going. This brings me to a very crucial point. Where exactly are you going? Answer: where there are other people. Head for any well-lit public place where there are large groups of people, shops or department stores, petrol stations, or better still the police station, if you can. But do not even think about running home. If you are being chased, the last thing you want is for your pursuer to know where you live. Another crucial thing to remember is make a lot of noise while you are running, scream, shout 'Help!', 'Fire!', 'Rape!', anything you can think of to draw attention to your situation. Make as much noise as you possibly can. Unfortunately, human nature tends to make most people try to ignore this sort of disturbance. There is a tendency to turn the other way and pretend not to have

Don't sit with your legs crossed when travelling on public transport, keep your feet on the floor to keep your balance should you need to get up quickly

REACT REMINDER

seen or heard – it's the 'nothing to do with me' syndrome. Don't be ignored; if necessary force your attentions on somebody, preferably a group or family. You can always apologise later if you are sure you are out of danger.

There is absolutely no shame in running away. It is a perfectly acceptable defensive strategy. For the male of the species it may not do the ego much good at the time, but just remember that some of the bravest and most brilliant military strategists throughout history have advocated a retreat or tactical withdrawal at some time, or to put it another way, good, old-fashioned running away! Call it what you will, it is often the right and most sensible thing to do. One thing for women to consider is high-heeled shoes – get rid of them. Kick them off before you start to run or while you are running. However, if possible, try to hold onto at least one of them as it could be a useful improvised weapon.

FIGHT

You have tried to talk your way out, to no avail. You seem to have no means of escape. The situation is getting uglier. What are you going to do now? Your third and final option is to fight. This is the last thing you want, but at this stage there is no

I will not be your victim

alternative apart from give up, become a victim and let this person rob, rape or even kill you. But what do we say to that?

NO! I don't think so. I will not be a victim today, thank you very much!

REACT
REMINDER >> If you are in danger of being raped remember that the attacker is at his most vulnerable with his trousers down

R
E
A
C
T

You may not even have had the luxury of choosing between dialogue or running away. What about sudden violence, the surprise attack or ambush? There's been no time to talk and you are in the thick of it straight away although if you had been following the **REACT** system, theoretically you should never be surprised by a sudden attack, but shit happens. So, you are going to fight! What now?

Don't be negative, you can do this. You don't have to be a black belt, you don't have to be muscle-bound. Yes you, little old you, can fight and you *will* survive. I will go into more detail in the following two sections, but there are some basic concepts that you should understand.

ENTRY

You must enter your attacker's intimate zone in order to engage. You must take the initiative and take the fight to him. Overwhelm the situation with your indignity and be totally focused on striking first.

Become the predator

Women should try to overcome their fear of fighting. Many women are fitter and quicker than their male counterparts and have great reserves of strength and determination

REACT REMINDER

R
E
A
C
T

SURPRISE

The essence of success is surprise. The last person in the world to know what you're going to do should be your attacker. Let out a blood-curdling scream as you move in. Spit in his face if necessary. Put him on his back foot. Do not give him a chance to recover as you enter his space and strike.

CONTACT

Make contact first with as much power as you can muster, but do not rely on one blow, keep on going until you are sure you are safe.

COUNTER

When contact is first made there is a likelihood that blows will be exchanged, especially if your first blow was not effective. Remember, he should be on the defensive and moving backward. Even if you get hit, press your attack home, keep on going.

DISENGAGE

Know when to stop. Pull back and evaluate the situation. If you are satisfied that you are no longer in danger, get away, but if there is a possibility that he may keep coming, attack again. Until you are safe you must continue to pursue him. However, it is not your place to punish your attacker – that is the job of the law. It is entirely up to you whether you leave the scene or restrain him and call the authorities. Do what you think is right. Only do what is within the law but ensure, above all, that you are safe.

About 90 per cent of self-defence is about learning how to recognise potential violence and thereby, hopefully avoiding it. The other 10 per cent, unfortunately, relies on physical action or fighting. Keep in mind, real fights are ugly. They tend not to last very long but, in a relatively short space of time, there can be an extreme amount of violence. Avoid them like the plague. But, if you do have to fight to protect yourself, your loved ones or your property, *fight like a tiger.* Don't even think about losing. Give yourself permission to take over and terminate your aggressor.

R
E
A
C
T

REACT REMINDER ▶▶ If you are confronted by a knife attacker who is making stabbing movements at you, try to take the blade on your briefcase or handbag

THE LAW

You are not going to get into trouble with the law by talking your way out of a situation or by running away. However, you should be aware of where you stand legally when you have to defend yourself physically. You need to make yourself familiar with the laws in your own country or state, and if you travel regularly, those of the countries or states you visit.

Without getting into pages of legal jargon, the overall thinking on self-defence is very similar wherever you are, depending on whether or not it is legal to carry a weapon. Basically, the law says that *every person has the right to protect themselves from attack, and if deemed necessary, to act in self defence of others, on condition that no more force is used than that which could be considered reasonable to repel an attack. Such force would not be considered an offense under common law. Also, a person who believes they are about to be attacked does not have to wait until the attack has happened before defending themselves. If the circumstances are as dire as they perceive them to be, a pre-emptive strike may be justified.*

Seems simple enough, but who decides what is reasonable force? It's that word *reasonable*. Reasonable to whom? You? Your attacker? The law? It's open to interpretation. This subject is vast and could be a whole book in its own right, but the bottom line is, once again, it's down to you on the day. Only you will know what your perception of the danger is. Reasonable force could mean push him aside and run away, or take his life before he takes yours. No-one can tell you, not even the law.

It is your responsibility to get it right.

R
E
A
C
T

If you have a dog, let it sleep at the top of the stairs and allow it to roam freely in the house at night ≫ **REACT** REMINDER

Let's look at it positively. The law is clear. You have the right to defend yourself. You have the right to use whatever force you deem to be reasonable under the circumstances. If you perceive that you are in immediate danger, a pre-emptive strike is not unlawful. So, do whatever you believe you have to do to stay safe, and justify it later. However, if the police are involved, stay calm, show them respect and do as they ask you. Try not to hinder them as they are doing an extremely difficult job. Think very carefully about what you say because it could be used as evidence at a later date. Also, take into consideration that to a police officer you may initially appear to be the bad guy. He could totally misunderstand the situation, particularly if you have used an improvised weapon to defend yourself. Do not get into an argument and start showing aggression, even if you know the officer has got it wrong. Be polite and co-operative. Wait for the proper time to explain what really happened.

MAKESHIFT AND IMPROVISED WEAPONS

In many parts of the world it is a criminal offense to carry a weapon of any description for the purpose of self-defence. However, there are situations, especially if you believe your life is in danger, when the use of a weapon may be necessary. In fact, in certain instances, using a weapon may be your only practical option in order to survive and an improvised or makeshift weapon may be the only answer. Almost anything you can hold in your hand can be used as a weapon. On the spur of the moment everyday household items can be used or converted into formidable, makeshift weapons. Objects not normally thought of as weapons are more often than not close at hand. Quick thinking, a little imagination and almost anything will do.

I wouldn't recommend that anyone actually carries a weapon. As I have already said, guns, knives, chemical sprays, stun guns and so on are illegal in most countries. It is more than possible that you can end up in more serious trouble with the law than your attacker for

REACT REMINDER >> If you encounter an incident on the street such as a fight or an arrest, don't become a spectator and put yourself at risk

defending yourself with an illegal weapon. There is a good argument that says if you carry a knife, for instance, you may just be looking for trouble and not have it purely for self-defence purposes. The same principle applies to other objects used as weapons – a hammer, a beer bottle, a crowbar. If you have them on your person for the sole purpose of using them as a weapon or doing another person harm, you have committed an offense and the law will take its course. The law clearly identifies a weapon as: *any article made or adapted to cause injury to, or incapacitate a person, to destroy or damage property or intended by the person having it with them for such use, whether by them or another person.*

However, everyday objects may have to be pressed into service in what you perceive to be a life or death emergency situation. Find out what the law allows you to carry legally in your country or state for self-defence purposes. If the answer is 'nothing' and, as we all know, the law does not apply to the criminal factions,

Almost anything can be used as a weapon

R
E
A
C
T

Remember everyday items such as pens and combs can be used to protect yourself

≪ REACT
REMINDER

which means that a would-be assailant could be carrying a weapon, thus putting you at a great disadvantage. Under these circumstances you may have to arm yourself and there are many everyday items that you can justify the possession of if challenged by a police officer. Picture the courtroom scene: 'Yes, your honour, my client admits to inflicting severe lacerations to Mr Jones' face, but he was viciously attacked with a large knife and defended himself with a plastic credit card.' Whose side do you think the jury might just be on? Speaking of juries, there is a saying used by special forces units which goes

▶▶ 'IT IS BETTER TO BE JUDGED BY TWELVE THAN CARRIED BY SIX'.

Makes sense, doesn't it? So don't carry a weapon that is obviously a weapon, but be aware that you are surrounded by objects that can be used as weapons when absolutely necessary.

A small selection of improvised weapons in use

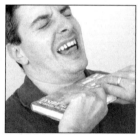
Jamming the edge of a book into the windpipe

Stabbing a pen into the neck

Raking the hard bristles of a brush across the face

Striking under the chin with the heel of a shoe

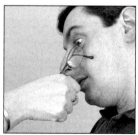
Poking the eyes with a pair of spectacles

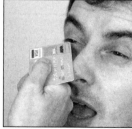
Slashing the eyes with the edge of a credit card

REACT REMINDER ➤➤ Consider carrying a whistle or some kind of personal alarm, especially if out walking alone

Striking the face with a
bunch of keys

Striking the eyes with a
mobile phone

Raking the face with an
ice-scraper

Spraying cleaning fluid or
aerosol into the face

Fending off with a mop or
a brush

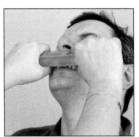

Striking under the nose with
any small, hard object

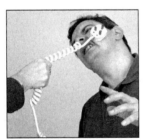

Using electrical flex as a flail

Striking with a picture frame
or any ornament

Fending off an attack with a
chair

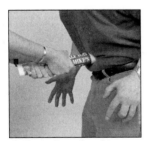

Strike to the solar plexus
with a rolled up newspaper

Hooking a coat hanger into
the mouth or nostrils

Slamming a handbag into
the face

**When approaching your parked car always have
your keys ready in your hand**   **《 REACT REMINDER**

R
E
A
C
T

REACT ▶

CONCENTRATE

Pretty much everything we do in our lives requires a certain amount of concentration to one degree or another, whether at work or at play. Some of our concentrational powers are subliminal so that although you are concentrating you are not consciously aware of it. The simple act of walking, putting one foot in front of the other, is a classic example. With every step you take there is a point just before you put your leading foot on the ground, when your whole body is totally off-balance, and if your subliminal concentration did not counteract this off-balance state, you would fall flat on your face. If the ground were suddenly moved from under your leading foot it would be just like stepping off the edge of a cliff. Your unconscious concentration on walking stops you falling over.

We are all concentrating on something all the time. A more obvious form of focused concentration is the psyching-up for competitive sport as when an athlete focuses all their mental and physical powers in one direction. The will to win is one of the most basic psychological traits in all of us and is just as important, if not more so, than skill or technique. Without the correct mental attitude and totally focused concentration your skill level is irrelevant. Watch the athletes in the Olympic Games. They are the best in the world and you can almost taste the intensity of their concentration. For example, watch a typical powerlifter prowl up and down like a lion in front of the barbell. That weight is his sworn enemy. He hates it and he is not going to let it beat him. He stares at it, shouting and

Don't put your purse or wallet in the top of a shopping bag where it is visible to passers-by

REACT
REMINDER

R
E
A
C
T

cursing. His coach will urge him on, slapping his face and shoulders, building the aggression into a crescendo so that at the point when he grips that steel bar, his physical and mental powers are so concentrated that the only two things in the world are him and the weight. He has cultivated the will to win, to lift that weight high above his head in triumphant glory.

It is your determination and your will to win and, more to the point, your will to survive, that will enable you to successfully defend yourself – not your strength or skill. You could be the most knowledgeable self-defence person in the world, but without the right mental attitude, the will to survive and a capacity to focus your concentration, you will lose.

IT IS DETERMINATION AND THE WILL TO WIN THAT MAKES A CHAMPION.

There is always a certain amount of skill required, but the one thing all winners have in common is their mental ability to concentrate and focus to the exclusion of everything else. Do not ignore the psychological element of self-defence, your personal protection is your responsibility and when you are required to terminate a situation you have to feel 200 per cent confident that you are going to win and walk away safely.

BEING STRONG

There are two kinds of strength, the outer and the inner. Our outer strength is the most obvious. Physical fitness and muscular development are something we should all be concerned with, and you owe it to yourself to keep as fit as you can. But this is not a book on diet, keep fit or how to build big biceps!

Physical fitness and strength will diminish with age. They are also dependent on your natural build, your inherited physical traits, which could have endowed you with strengths or weaknesses, and of course your age and sex. Although we are able to improve our physical

R
E
A
C
T

REACT REMINDER >> When you stop at traffic lights always keep your car in gear, ready to drive away quickly if you need to

fitness and stature, the majority of us are what we are and are pretty much stuck with it. If you are concerned with your physical fitness and general well-being, that's great. If, however, you're simply not interested in developing your outer strength, you do have to consider your inner strength as it is this part of your make-up that is crucial as far as self-defence and personal protection are concerned.

Developing your muscles and fighting skills are not as essential as developing psychological strength.

In a physical confrontation stress and fear are your biggest enemies, not the actual aggressor. You will be attacked psychologically well before there is a physical attack, and the overwhelming stress of an attack can be so mentally debilitating that you will freeze. Whether you have 8-inch or 18-inch biceps will make absolutely no difference whatsoever!

The psychological attack

If you are under extreme stress it is possible to go deaf, to lose all sense of time, to go colour blind, develop tunnel vision and lose co-ordination of fine motor skills. In fact all normal perception can be distorted. How many times have you heard someone talk about an accident they have been involved in and say that everything seemed to be happening in slow motion? This is typical of an extreme stress-induced distortion of perception. Understanding what is happening to you is the key to dealing with it and then turning it into an ally.

Always have your house key in your hand ready for use when you come home

R
E
A
C
T

MOTIVATION UNDER STRESS

We have already said that stress can be one of your biggest enemies – if you let it. First of all, let's not pretend that stress won't be present, because it will. But remember, you are using the principles of **REACT** and you have already recognised and evaluated the situation. Your main aim now is to concentrate all your mental and physical powers. Before we move on, ask yourself a couple of very simple questions:

Am I willing to let this person rob, rape, beat, cripple, blind or even kill me?

Do I think it is acceptable to let this person take away my property or even more, my ability to work or play, and therefore no longer be able to support my family or continue to live and enjoy the rest of my life to the full?

I hope that when you said '**NO**' it lifted the roof!

NO! You will not enter my life!

NO! I will not be your victim!

NO! I will not die today!

Feel angry? Feel motivated?
Good! So you should!

Show your indignation - get angry

These people should not have the right to breathe the same air as you, let alone prey on you. Consolidate in your mind all those things that make your life worth living. Keep it personal: it's your stuff, they're your kids, it's your life!

It's amazing how the stress will dissipate when you become motivated. Your indignity and determination not to be a victim will trigger an adrenaline rush, which will turn you into a warrior with a

REACT REMINDER >> When in an unfamiliar building, always locate your escape route as a matter of course

mind-set that says, 'I will not die today, no matter how big my attacker is. I will terminate this situation to my advantage.'

THE ADRENALINE RUSH

The adrenaline glands are like little caps which are situated at the top of each kidney. If you are under stress, angry or frightened, these glands secrete a cocktail of natural hormones into your system. These hormones are released to help you cope with emergencies. Your blood pressure will rise, your heart rate will increase and the sugar content of your blood will rise dramatically. Your spleen contracts and produces a reserve amount of blood into your system. The adrenaline glands also stimulate the conversion of proteins into carbohydrates, thus increasing your energy, and regulate the levels of potassium and sodium which have the effect of magnifying the feelings of aggression, which in turn, increase your pain threshold.

All that sounds a bit medical but the bottom line is, when you are feeling stressed or frightened it is because of the chemicals that are being released into your body, and those chemicals are your allies.

FEAR IS YOUR FRIEND

It is possible to be totally paralysed with fear. Think of a rabbit caught in a car's headlights. Fear is a perfectly natural, emotional state of mind, just like anger or sorrow. Without it we would all put ourselves in positions of extreme danger all the time and, as a result, probably not live very long. Those who say that they are not frightened of anything are either plain liars, deluding themselves or simply particularly stupid. Most of us will think of fear as a negative and, if not understood and managed, it can be devastating.

If you allow fear to terrorise you it will control your actions.

An attacker is relying on your fear of him to create confusion

R
E
A
C
T

Avoid parking your car near bushes and shrubs which could conceal an attacker

REACT
REMINDER

The author faces his fear

and panic and therefore diminish the effectiveness of your response. Fear is an emotion that can cause some of us to act more violently than we would normally and that can have sad consequences. We all have fears, many of them irrational but nevertheless very, very real to those who have them such as fear of snakes, spiders, heights, the dentist and so on. What may seem stupid to one person to another is a real problem and, of course, if being afraid of snakes keeps you away from them that's probably no bad thing for that person. However, if faced with a snake or, in our case our potentially violent or confrontational situation, you must try to understand that the overwhelming feeling of fear is actually a positive emotion. You must try to embrace the fear and recognise that the feelings you are experiencing, both mentally and physically, are your friends and will help you.

FEAR ACTIVATES A SURVIVAL MECHANISM IN US ALL.

When you are frightened the adrenaline glands dump that cocktail of hormones into the bloodstream, which summons up reserves of power and strength. Your muscles tense in order to ward off an attack, your breathing rate will rapidly increase to supply more oxygen to your body, your heart rate increases to supply more blood to your muscles and you will break out in a cold sweat which has the effect of cooling the body but warming the muscles ready for action. So, while you are feeling like shit, and wanting to throw up, your body is saying, 'Come on then, I'm ready to fight!' Make the most of what nature has given you. Fear is your friend. You must breathe through the rush of adrenaline that surges through your system. Focus your mind and co-ordinate the energy.

REACT REMINDER >> Avoid visiting unattended service premises such as laundrettes alone at night

Inhale forcibly through your nose and breathe out as slowly as you can through your mouth. Repeat this exercise if you have time. I am not telling you to fight, but your body is telling you that if you can't get away, it is able to fight and never more so than now. You can feel this physically happening: your senses will become more acute and you can hear your own heart beat. None of this makes you feel good at the time, but it is all a major contribution to your survival. Don't be put off by the fact that you feel bad, you feel apprehensive, your mouth is dry, you may start to tremble and your voice may become broken and high pitched because these are all natural responses to the situation. You must work through them. Remember, the things you feel are the result of chemicals being released into your system. Yes, you are frightened but it's OK to be scared. Just try to put it into perspective. Although it is a cliché, it is nevertheless true that the only thing to fear is fear itself if you think of fear as a negative. The opposite is actually the case and fear is a positive emotion if you understand what's happening to you. As I have said, fear is your friend.

YOUR MIND AS A WEAPON

Of all the weapons you have at your disposal, such as your hands, feet, elbows, knees, plus all the other stuff at hand such as chairs, books, bottles and sticks etc., the most powerful weapon you have in your arsenal is, in fact, between your ears.

▶▶ **YOUR MIND CONTROLS YOUR BODY.**

As I have said before, you will be attacked psychologically long before any physical contact is made and, therefore, your initial defence will be triggered psychologically. It is understandable that most of us think in terms of only having one brain inside our heads. In fact we actually have three brains. As each of our evolutionary phases took place, a new brain was born and placed over the top of

Try to remain calm if you are attacked by a mugger - remember he is probably as nervous as you are

REACT REMINDER

the old one, and by the time our modern cognitive brain was in place, our previous two brains, the reptilian and mammalian brains, had become locked away in the dark recesses of our minds but were nevertheless still there. Obviously these brains were not as sophisticated as our modern one, but they still play a significant part in all our lives. The first, and therefore the oldest, is our reptilian brain. This is the one we are primarily concerned with for the **REACT** system, because this brain still controls the human survival mechanisms. The middle brain, or mammalian brain, is the one used by all animals other than humans. The reptilian brain is pure instinct, no thought, no expression, no fear, just survival. A reptile does only what it has to in order to survive, and that is exactly what we ought to do in a self-defence situation. Imagine a big, old

Don't mess with me

alligator lying on a riverbank in the midday sun. He just wants to be left alone to mind his own business and to live his life, but go too close, or worse still mess with him, and he will kill you. He won't stop to consider any moral or legal implications. He won't back off or run away as a mammal might. No, he will just kill you then go back to lying in the sun as if nothing had ever happened. Now, we still have this reptilian instinct in our heads, but our modern, cognitive brain is so prevalent that we have forgotten how to use our older instincts. So what we need to do is to tap in to our reptilian

Keep packages and handbags on the floor of your vehicle, not on the front seat where they are an open invitation to a 'smash and grab' robbery

brain and try to think like an animal when necessary. Animals don't plan self-defence moves; the alligator isn't lying there in the sun thinking about what to if someone attacked him, but if you are stupid enough to get inside his intimate zone he will instinctively strike you pre-emptively. Sounds familiar? Unfortunately, we do have to think about what to do if somebody attacks us, but just being aware that you still have the ability to react instinctively is a step in the right direction to subconsciously focusing your mind into a formidable weapon,

Focus your mind

triggering your brain into reptilian mode. Once locked in, even the smallest, weakest, most unlikely person will be capable of defending themselves like a wild animal. Nothing to do with skill, nothing to do with the size of your muscles but everything to do with your mind!

Your mental attitude towards self-defence can be so overwhelming and powerful that you must not allow yourself to go into a negative state of mind. In other words, you must not defeat yourself before you have even started. Your mind is your most powerful weapon, but if you allow it, your mind can also be your most formidable opponent. Your thoughts must motivate your actions. Don't allow fear to cloud your mind. Fear is not your enemy. All negative thoughts must be driven out of your head. Talk to yourself in a positive and assertive manner, 'I will not lose', 'I will not fail'. 'So what if it hurts a bit? I will walk away from this, I will not be beaten and I will certainly never give up, whatever happens.' Talk to that old alligator that's lurking somewhere in the dark recesses of your mind, he won't let you down. Your will to survive is the most important weapon in your arsenal.

R
E
A
C
T

Don't throw envelopes or other documents showing your name and address into public rubbish bins

REACT REMINDER

BECOME THE PREDATOR

You must take the attitude that you will not, under any circumstances whatsoever, become a victim. In fact, faced with a potentially nasty situation, you will indeed become the predator and not the prey. Being a predator may seem a little alien to you, especially when we are talking about self-defence. The point is that your mind-set should be that of the superior being. You must have the conviction to apply whatever methods you deem necessary to terminate a situation without a flicker of hesitation. Think of yourself as being higher up the food chain than this piece of scum attempting to invade your life and turn them into your prey. As I have previously said, if you only really have two choices in a potentially violent situation, fight or run away, then run away immediately or fight immediately. If you do run, run like a cheetah, but if you have to fight, fight like a tiger – like a predator.

What do all predators have in common? They attack, they do not defend. They are the aggressors and that just happens to be your assailant's worst nightmare. If he thought for one second that you were going to successfully fight back, he would not have considered attacking you in the first place.

▶▶ **You must give yourself permission to take the fight to him.**

Attack first and last. Then you will be ahead of the game. By invading his intimate space and attacking him for even thinking that you were going to be his victim, you have become the predator and he has become the prey. You must launch your pre-emptive strike at the first signal of his impending attack. Getting in first is crucial. Snap instantly into a predatory state of mind. Move in with swift and powerful combinations of strikes and blows. Show no mercy to what is now your prey.

The predator knows it is going to win before it starts an attack.

**R
E
A
C
T**

REACT REMINDER ⟩⟩ Don't be intimidated by nuisance or obscene telephone callers. Keep a loud whistle by the phone and don't be frightened to use it!

Knowledge is power and your power comes from the knowledge that you are not going to be beaten. In fact, you can't be beaten because you aren't going to give your assailant the chance to beat you. They are the terrorist, you are the SAS.

Action will always, without exception, beat reaction, therefore attack is and always has been the best means of defence. Please don't get me wrong, I am not trying to turn you into a thug no better than the types we are trying to avoid, but we are talking about survival and you must remember we are not dealing with nice, rational and reasonable people. That being so, and as the dictionary definition of pre-emptive says *'effectively destroying the enemy or the enemy's weapons before they can be used against you,* what's wrong with forestalling that hostile action if it was going to be directed at you? See how hitting first suddenly seems to be quite acceptable and not such a bad idea! Go with your gut feelings. If you are uncomfortable with a situation, certain that you are in danger, but uncertain when an attack will come although convinced that it will, take over. Become the predator. Pre-empt the situation and terminate any way you have to.

Show no mercy

Keep your car doors locked at all times and never have the windows open wide enough to allow a thief to get his/her hand in

REACT REMINDER

R E A C T

DESCRIBING AN ASSAILANT

Could you describe an assailant to the police if you had to? You need to construct a clear mental picture of exactly what happened and a concise description of the person.

▶▶ **IT IS MORE IMPORTANT TO REMEMBER THEIR CHARACTERISTICS THAN THEIR CLOTHING.**

Particular attention should be paid to those characteristics that cannot be changed such as scars, tattoos, physical mannerisms, etc.

With a little practice you can train yourself to accurately identify a person after seeing them for only a few seconds. Try a little exercise, the next time you are sitting in a doctor's waiting room or on a train, look at someone for a few seconds then look away. Close your eyes and list the characteristics you can recall. This may seem trivial at that moment but remember, one day you may have to answer pertinent questions just like these. You may be in shock or even injured, and the last thing you will want to do is answer questions, but you have to focus your mind on the most accurate description you can give to assist the police. They may just catch the guy! You got away but the next person may not be so lucky.

The following diagram shows how all the salient features and characteristics of a person can be categorised in a logical format. Look at the diagram and systematically move down the body from the head to the feet. Don't worry, you're not going to remember it all. However, the system of a logical progression from top to bottom will help you develop your own formula to remember a description. This, of course, does not just apply to self-defence or describing someone that may have attacked you; the same formula applies if you are a witness to any incident where you may be asked to give a description of those involved to the police.

R
E
A
C
T

REACT REMINDER ▶▶ Never assume that a stranger in uniform is legitimate - always check with their employer

DESCRIBING AN ASSAILANT

HEIGHT
very tall, tall, medium, short, very short

EARS
large, small, jug, small lobes, large lobes, earrings, cauliflower

FACE SHAPE
round, square, oval, long, fat, thin

SCARS
arm, leg, hand, wrist, neck, chest, back, disfigurement due to burns etc.

COMPLEXION
skin colour, spots, scars, birthmarks, moles, warts, dirty, fresh-faced

BUILD
heavy, light, stocky, skinny, athletic, chubby, fat

TATOOS
hands, arms, shoulders, patterns, pictures, names, words, initials

JEWELLERY
rings, bracelets, necklaces, badges, initials

CLOTHES
colour, garments, neat, untidy, lettering, logos, patches, tears, missing buttons, gloves, uniform, workwear

ACCESSORIES
were they holding anything – bag, weapon, car keys?

FOOTWEAR
colour, shoes, boots, trainers, sandals, high heels, unusual design, large, small

HAIR
colour, long, short, curly, straight, clean, greasy, receding, thick, bald, wig, afro, moustache, beard, sideburns

EYEBROWS
heavy, thin, none, meeting in the middle

EYES
colour, glasses, cross-eyed, false eye, bulging, squint

NOSE
small, large, aquiline, bulbous, broken, hooked, roman

TEETH
missing, gold, broken, false, decayed, irregular, protruding, stained, overbite

VOICE
loud, soft, accent, speech impediment, stutter, stammer, repeated use of any words, unusual words, angry, refined or unrefined

DEFORMITIES
disfigured, hunchback, amputee, club foot

SEX
male, female, transexual, transvestite

AGE
sometimes difficult to assess

GAIT
striding, limp, bow-legged, limp, twine-toed

DIRECTION
which way did he/she/they go?

R
E
A
C
T

REACT

TERMINATE

On the front cover of this book I say 'Think Safe, Act Safe, Stay Safe' with the **REACT** approach to self-defence. Staying safe or 'surviving' is the main goal. No-one actually wins in a real fight, you only survive. Winning or losing is an ego thing, so to terminate a situation means to select an option that enables you to survive, and as I have said many times throughout this book, that could be as simple as running away. So please, for God's sake, don't let the word 'terminate' conjure up images of Arnold Schwarzenegger destroying everything in his path. If you are convinced that someone is about to do you serious bodily harm, get away. Run as fast as your little legs will carry you and leave the heroics to the likes of Arnie!

However, terminate could also mean the use of friendly or humourous dialogue. Talking can sometimes do the trick. Reason, diplomacy, tact and a little psychology can go a long way. All these things can and do work if the circumstances are right, but only you can judge what to do on the day.

As we all know, shit happens and if you can't get away or talk your way out immediately, and you are in the thick of it, you will have to resolve the situation with some kind of physical action. This section is dedicated to your fight option – 'the last resort'. We have explored all our other options in the previous chapters, therefore terminate, as far as we are now concerned, means you are going to have to fight. You didn't want to and in fact you did everything in

R
E
A
C
T

Carry a pocket-sized high intensity torch with you so you can illuminate dark areas if you need to **REACT REMINDER**

your power to avoid it, but to no avail. The time has come to eliminate all those negative thoughts.

What if it hurts? What if I lose?

You are in Condition Red. You are taking over this situation now!

Strike first!

As action will always beat reaction, you must strike first. 'But that's not self-defence,' I hear you cry. Rubbish! You are not dealing with nice, honest and reasonable people. Remember, you must now become the predator. You must take the fight to them, in other words, pre-empt their actions. If you have read all the signs and truly believe that this person in front of you is about to attack at any moment, give yourself permission to take the initiative. Why should you give them the courtesy of fighting on their terms? Why fight when they are ready to? Why fight when they want to? Take charge of the situation before you lose control of it.

▶▶ SUN-TZU (*Art of War*) WRITES 'THE HEIGHT OF STRATEGY IS TO ATTACK YOUR OPPONENT'S STRATEGY.'

In simple language, smack him before he smacks you! You only have two choices, to either leave now or fight now, and if for whatever reason you can't leave, then fight. Do it fast, do it first and do it hard! There are no rules. There is nothing sporting about self-preservation, especially when it involves dangerous individuals with criminal intent. Become the predator, show your assailant that you are more at home in this situation than they are by taking the initiative and attacking. The confrontation will be over with much sooner. Invading your opponent's intimate zone and leaping right down his throat gives you the advantage.

▶▶ TAKE CONTROL, BECOME THE PREDATOR.

Don't be overconfident, however. Always assume that your assailant is a vastly superior fighter than yourself, but your strategy

REACT REMINDER ▶▶ If you are being followed, don't go home unless you are certain that help is there

is that you are not going to give him a chance to show you. Smother his actions and stop his attack before it happens. You must launch your own pre-emptive strike at the first sign of an impending attack.

▶▶ **GETTING IN FIRST ISN'T JUST IMPORTANT, IT'S CRUCIAL!**

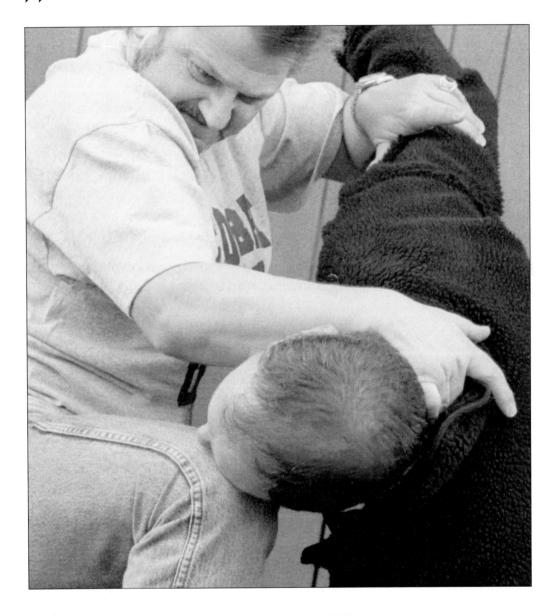

If you find yourself the target of aggression or aggravation in a public place such as a pub, don't stay and argue it out, just leave   《 **REACT** REMINDER

R
E
A
C
T

NOT LIKE OTHER BOOKS

By now you will have realised that **REACT** is like no other book you may have read on the subject of self-defence. For one thing, you won't find any of those 'how to do it' sequences of photographs and instructions on how to defend yourself against pre-determined attacks like the following:

What to do if you are grabbed by the throat from the front.

Attacker attempts to choke you with both hands from the front

Slap or punch the face to distract your attacker

Grip the sleeves under the elbows, push up on the right elbow and pull down and forward on the left elbow

Step across their body with your right foot and place it in front of their right foot

Bend your knees then quickly straighten your legs and sharply pull, throwing them over your right hip

Jerk their right arm upwards and dislocate the elbow joint over your knee while simultaneously striking their face

REACT
REMINDER 〉〉 If someone tries to get into your car at traffic lights drive away sounding your horn and flashing your lights, even if it means driving through a red light

Good defence technique or complete bullshit? Well, in fact there's nothing wrong with it. It's a very good jujutsu technique and it can work – if you have a spare lifetime to practice it! Martial arts techniques like this require a high skill level that is only attained with years of training. They rely on total coordination, balance, fine motor skills and muscle memory. They will not work for you on the street! You cannot learn self-defence techniques such as these from a book. Although the sequence of photographs shows a perfectly valid technique, no matter how good the photographs are, no matter how well the description of the mechanics of the technique are written, it cannot and never will be able to depict the realism of an actual attack.

When you practice with a friend or partner, you know they are not really going to strangle you to death, so learning techniques is a bit like learning to dance – you learn the moves in conjunction with a consenting partner. You may even perfect the move so that it looks absolutely magnificent when you perform it, and that's precisely the point, it's only a performance, not real life! Trying to learn techniques from a book is a waste of time. Learning martial arts techniques at your local club is a great thing to be involved in, but most of the time what you learn is not relevant to a street situation. When you practice your moves you know exactly when an attack is coming, how hard it will be and that your partner will comply with your actions in order not to get hurt. You know you will pull back or even miss on purpose so as not to injure your friend. It's not real and it never will be.

In real life the attack will look and feel totally different. It will be harder, faster and more brutal. There will be a massive and overwhelming psychological effect on your system and the attack may be accompanied by a tirade of verbal obscenities. Your attacker might spit in your face, you will be able to smell his breath and feel his finger nails digging into your flesh. This guy is in your face and he is trying to choke the life out of you. Do you honestly believe you will have the time to think of the hundreds of techniques you have read about or been shown at the club, select the right one and execute it effectively with speed and accuracy? I don't think so!

Kidding yourself that you can learn this stuff from a book, not to mention martial arts instructors kidding you that learning complex classical techniques for a couple of hours on a Tuesday night will save your life one day is bullshit. And it's dangerous bullshit! It lulls you into a false sense of security. Remember, all that coordination and fine motor skill count for nothing when you are out of the safe environment of the training hall. This guy is not your friend; he intends to be the predator and you are his prey. It doesn't matter how well you have learned your dance routine because it won't help you here. So, I will not show you any complex techniques because techniques do not win fights.

Quick, simple and effective

Let's go back and look at the photographs of that jujutsu technique again. Take a good look and ask yourself a couple of simple questions. Why the hell did she allow the guy to grab her by the throat in the first place? A person so intent on doing you harm would have displayed all the danger signs well in advance of the physical attack. Also, if she has time to slap him in the face to distract him in order to execute the full technique, she definitely has time to gouge him in the eyes and run away. Who needs all the other stuff? So, if I'm not going to show you self-defence techniques, what am I going to show you?

**R
E
A
C
T**

REACT >> **REMINDER** >>   Only use public lavatories when absolutely necessary

THE TOOLS

As I've said, techniques don't win fights. Knowledge and an understanding of what is happening to you and why, an accurate evaluation of a situation and the ability to give yourself permission to take control – that's what wins fights. That's what will help you to survive.

Remember our tool box with those five drawers? All the equipment you need is in there somewhere. You just have to find the right tool, or combination of tools, that will enable you to do the job. All the equipment is right there under your nose: some of it you will like, some of it you won't while some of it may not suit your natural abilities. Choose the tools that you think will work for you. Build your own system of personal protection. Only you know how fast, strong or aggressive you can be, but you may surprise yourself when under attack. Only you will know what's right for you on the day.

Construct defensive strategies that you feel confident with. For instance, you wouldn't try to knock a nail in with a screwdriver would you? The same logic applies to self-defence and if you choose the right tool for the job, it will work. If he's 6'3" and you're 4'10" you wouldn't try to grab him by the hair or kick him in the teeth, but you could go for his ankles, knees or groin. And remember, even if he is 6'3" and built like a bear, his ankles are no stronger than yours. You must use what you think will work for you.

You are what you are! Okay, so you're not built like Hercules, you don't have 27 black belts to your name – so what? You can use what you have and take advantage of your natural abilities. If you don't think you have any, you are wrong. Everybody can defend themselves. Remember you, and only you, are responsible for your own safety and believe me, you are up to the task. Let's look at some of the stuff that even you can do.

R
E
A
C
T

Never load your car with luggage etc. the night before you leave, always load it in the morning

Some things to consider when building up your own arsenal are:

- *How much skill does it require?*
- *Will it work against anybody, no matter how big or strong they are?*
- *Could I do it under stress?*
- *Is it easy to remember?*
- *Am I capable of delivering it effectively?*

Techniques don't win fights – you already know that – but concepts and strategies do, especially when based on your natural reactions and abilities. One of the most effective and innovative theories based around this principle is the S.P.E.A.R. SYSTEM™.

THE S.P.E.A.R. SYSTEM™

The S.P.E.A.R. is a concept that utilises the body's natural propensity to flinch as a response to danger or shock. This concept has been developed by a Canadian friend and colleague, Tony Blauer. He has spent more than 20 years researching, studying and refining his conflict management and combat survival concepts. Tony is, without doubt, one of the most innovative and skillful practical martial arts instructors around today and his psychological approach to self-defence has been proven time and time again. He has instructed police, military and Special Forces personnel in his concepts of the S.P.E.A.R. SYSTEM™, the Panic Attack and HIGH GEAR Simulation suit and the 'stun and run' theory all over the world. Tony's work dovetails so perfectly into my **REACT** system and, because the tactics and philosophies we both advocate seem to run almost in parallel, he has agreed to share some of his theories with the readers of this book. I would heartily recommend that you visit Tony on his web site www.tonyblauer.com for a further insight to this remarkable man's work.

R E A C T

REACT REMINDER >> Walk on the side of the street facing the oncoming traffic. That way you can't be approached by a vehicle from behind

So what is the S.P.E.A.R. SYSTEM™? Throughout our lives we have all been taught to move away from danger and in fact it is a basic instinct to recoil from any threat. However, in a real self-defence situation we should move 'tactically' towards the danger. Yes, we advocate running when you can, but unfortunately there are many situations where you could be attacked from very close range, such as a surprise attack, date rape, car jacking or violent mugging, where flight is not an option until you've dealt with your opponent.

It is for this extreme close quarter moment that the S.P.E.A.R. SYSTEM™ was designed. Remember, as humans, we recoil from danger, but tactically, the only way to stop it is to address it! That means move towards it! It is this paradox that creates hesitation and anxiety in most people. Why? Because there are two conflicting messages: *get away NOW* and *confront the problem*. The result is often what Tony refers to as 'emotional inertia' where a person's inability to move mentally will often result in an inability to move physically. The S.P.E.A.R. SYSTEM™ is a genetically inspired self-protection method which helps us to take advantage of our instinctive response to danger or attack. It exploits the natural responses of our intuitive survival system. It is completely natural and totally subconsciously triggered, and as a result it is incredibly fast.

Here's how and why it works. Your survival system has built-in radar that will identify danger and will instinctively attempt to protect you from attack. Your intuition and instincts combine to create a 'flinch response' that is designed to protect your body, in particular your head, or what Tony calls the 'command centre', from sudden impact. It is this flinch position that actually sets up your body's natural weapons, such as the elbow, forearm, nails, palms and so on. Remember, when you flinch, your arms come up with blinding speed. Now, if you can use that speed and position to your advantage, you are on your way to a classic 'stun-and-run' tactic.

R
E
A
C
T

If faced with a 'flasher' don't laugh or humiliate him, just ignore the man and report him to the police at your earliest opportunity

REACT
REMINDER

Tony's years of research indicate that there are three types of flinch responses. No matter who you are or how highly trained you may be, you will display these three 'moving away from danger' flinches:

- *Attacks from a distance are characterised by a pushing away gesture.*

- *Attacks from the front and up-close result in a covering and leaning-away posture.*

- *Attacks from very close in and off to one side result in a shielding and turning action.*

Therefore, as Tony rightly says, incorporating the flinch into our self-defence arsenal is the smartest thing we can do and here's why: like it or not you are going to flinch when you are attacked. It doesn't mean you're not well trained or even a coward. However, it does mean that you're not asleep and that your brain is working and your natural survival system is sending you a message. The flinch is a result of a stimulus being introduced too quickly into your brain, or that 'holy shit!' moment, as Tony would put it. Think of the times that you opened the door just as someone was about to ring the bell. You flinched! Yes, you did! You lurched back. What you didn't do, however, was to snap into a fighting stance like the Karate Kid, Bruce Lee or Jackie Chan. You flinched and that's good. It is crucial that you embrace the idea of the flinch response. It is not weakness. All it is is your natural survival system backing you up, telling you it's ready for action.

Okay, so what has your natural flinch response got to do with spears? Tony's system is important to us because it is based on your natural behaviour. He uses the 'spear' as a tactical icon, a spear being an impaling weapon which is thrust towards a opponent. This is crucial in motivating you to attack your attacker. But there's much more to the name. Tony Blauer's S.P.E.A.R. is

R E A C T

REACT REMINDER »» Never travel on the upper deck of a double-decker bus when you're alone. Always choose a seat downstairs where you can see your stop in advance

actually an acronym for 'Spontaneous Protection Enabling Accelerated Response'. Trying to understand exactly what that means is easier if you read Tony's own words:

Tony Blauer

Most of what martial artists practice in terms of self-defence is not real. The moment there is a contest there is awareness, which means there is preparation. These psychological components completely change your mindset. In a real situation there are so many emotional and psychological factors that the sensory overload can negate all those years of training. The remedy is to address the problem of how real fights occur and what is behaviourally realistic. In other words, you must proactively analyse how you are likely to move, act and think in a real assault and work around that model. Most people focus on the offensive, not the protective. In other words, they fixate on what they will do to the attacker, not on what he might do to them. This slight perspective shift is the difference between a proactive system that increases perception speed and decreases reaction time. My focus is on a very simple premise: real fights are not fun, real fights are messy and real fights are those confrontations in which emotionally we wish we were somewhere else.

Behaviourally, we all move away from danger, but tactically the only way to stop a physical threat at close quarters is by moving towards it. Real fights happen in the space of a telephone booth. The S.P.E.A.R. is the only behaviourally based self-defence system that analyses and uses the survival flinch response. In a true ambush moment your brain experiences a delay between stimulus and response, though in reality it's not a response, it's a reaction. This is the paradox of martial arts-based training. When we agree to fight someone we can mentally adjust and

R
E
A
C
T

respond, but when the attack is a real surprise we are more likely to react rather than respond and that is why I believe that my concept of the S.P.E.A.R. dovetails perfectly into Steve's REACT system. Terminate, or tactics as I would prefer to call it, is the doorway to the S.P.E.A.R. SYSTEM™.

For more than twenty years I've analysed the most common responses to surprise attacks and designed cognitive drills around them. Practice of these tactics will turn your natural flinch into a trigger to engage your close quarter arsenal. In other words, it helps you convert a reactive response into a real protective action. I have not invented a new style, but I have created a realistic and effective bridge to get you to a position where you can use a style if you've been trained in one, or launch a defence counterattack against an assailant, based on some of Steve's tactics or your own instinctive tactics. I like to remind people in my seminars of something very profound: 'There are more people in the world today with absolutely no training whatsoever who have successfully defended themselves using sheer will and indignation, than there ever will be trained martial artists who get attacked and successfully defend themselves!' Remember that. You are a survival organism and you can fight back and win using the S.P.E.A.R. SYSTEM™ and the REACT formula for safety.

As Steve has said throughout this book predators look for victims they can prey on. Use the principals of REACT and you should stay out of trouble. But, violence is a sad reality we must all address. Bluntly put, shit happens! An argument over a parking spot turns into a heated verbal exchange and bang, in comes the sucker punch and what happens? That's right, you flinch! By the sucker punch I mean any surprise attack such as a tackle, hair grab, anything. You have no knowledge of where or when an attack is coming, so trying to defend with a physical tactic is often too slow. The reason even trained people often fail is because most tactics are based on your anticipation of a specific physical attack. The attack is more likely to fail, not because you defended yourself technically, but because you flinched. Action is faster than reaction. When

REACT REMINDER » Never answer your phone with your own number. If you do receive a 'wrong number' telephone call, ask which number they were calling

an opponent attacks you they are already in action. Why the flinch works is that it is launched from the reactive portion in your brain's survival mechanism. The cognitive process is far too slow in a real fight.

In my studies and research I would find that individuals flinched more effectively than those that used martial art type movements. Shoulders would come up faster, hands would protect the face, ducking, twisting and intuitive and improvised movement was far faster than trying to block, counter or evade I realized that flinch speed, which we are all 'hand-wired' with, meaning it's part of our survival system, is faster than cognitive speed. That's identifying a threat and then mentally selecting the appropriate counter for it. Incredibly, the body is genetically wired to survive and we all have a built-in system waiting to be used in time of imminent danger!

Stand up now and pretend to flinch. Imagine someone has jumped you and grabbed your throat. Your hands explode upwards to protect your head. Now look at your position. Your palms are likely to be facing your imagined opponent's face. Your nails are poised to claw or rake. Your elbows may already be locked and loaded to deliver a savage strike. If you've been pushed off balance, you may now be poised to attack the groin or bladder area. In short, without studying a martial art, your flinch response has set you up for a devastating barrage of counter attacks. And you didn't even have to think about doing anything! All you need to do is trust your survival system. Of course deciding to 'fight back' is a cognitive choice at that moment. From the flinch you MUST turn yourself into the creature from Alien! Get right in the guy's face, knock him on his butt, give him a rebirthing experience so he's flashing back to being in his mother's womb and forgetting that he's a serial killer or a violent mugger. It's what Steve and I call the 'Predator/Prey Reversal'. Maybe that's a little dramatic, but the S.P.E.A.R. SYSTEM™ gives you that potential. As Steve says, become the predator. The only way to reverse the predator/prey relationship is to make the predator the prey. You must engage the threat, move in, fill the space and jam the attacker. Defend

If possible avoid walking with the traffic down a one way street. If you have no choice then walk on the driver's side of the vehicles - it will make it more difficult for a passenger to get out and grab you

REACT REMINDER

yourself from where you flinched, there's no need to reposition. Right in front of one of your natural weapons is a target - take it, think closest weapon, closest target. Think speed, stay loose, don't telegraph and explode from where you are.

Part of embracing the S.P.E.A.R. SYSTEM™ is in understanding that if you don't have prior knowledge that you will be attacked, as in prearranged sparring, a tournament, competition or a consenting street fight, your perception speed is minimal. That is, attacks in the martial arts school are emotionally slower because there is consent to fight one another. You're in the 'zone' as athletes like to say. The real street assault is different. Ask anybody who has been in a real explosive fight what the first thing he did was, and he'll say 'I don't know, it all happened so fast. All I knew was I was just hitting him in the head'. That's how it works. Somebody comes at you from just outside arm's reach for example, while you are having a verbal confrontation. The guy lunges, is it a shove, a choke or a punch? Who knows? Who cares? Who can actually see it at that moment and distance? And here's the point your reactive brain just screams 'Look out!'

Here's some more good stuff to store in the toolbox. The S.P.E.A.R. SYSTEM™ is what we've been discussing so far. The S.P.E.A.R. as a tactic is the actual physical position of your arms to form the shape of a diamond, ideally as you flinch. Again visualize an attack. Your hands come up to protect your head and your weight gets transferred to your back leg. You close your eyes and you turn away from the danger. Your attacker has actually put you in a perfect position for a tactical S.P.E.A.R. counter. Your hands are already up, your weight on the back foot. From that position power forward with a penetrating movement like a sling shot releasing you towards the threat. You are the human SPEAR, you must visualize this. Your hands must be outside 90 degrees for maximum strength so they form a triangle, which just happens to be one of the strongest geometric shapes in the world. Your arms create a natural barrier between the attack and your most vulnerable areas.

Because the S.P.E.A.R. is truly a genetically inspired system, it is something you don't have to study for years. Simply embracing it will allow you to use it. Of course, if you practice it from an instructional video, or get to one of our seminars you will be much better at it, but it really draws on the instincts and natural body mechanics we are all born with, and many have used it in real attacks without ever taking a formal lesson.

It's easy to get started with the S.P.E.A.R. and it's actually easier for the layperson to learn than for an instructor to teach. Why? Because the beginner has no muscle memory interfering with an instinctive reaction. Remember, it's based on how the body actually wants to move, not on how some animal moves or on reconfiguring your body into some sort of muscle-memory fighting stance. In other words it's spontaneous. Converting your flinch into a S.P.E.A.R. tactic changes everything in a self-defence moment because it provides you with the fastest and worst thing you can do to your opponent. That is to strike him pre-emptively in the last place that he is expecting to get hit. Tactically that's the best thing you could do, because you hurt him both physically and psychologically.

Let's recap some crucial ideas. Remember the flinch is triggered by the aggression of your attacker; the more aggression, the more you flinch. The more you flinch, the more you are like a coiled spring ready to power back with the S.P.E.A.R. You are spontaneously protecting yourself and that startle/flinch combination enables an accelerated response.

As I have said the S.P.E.A.R SYSTEM™ opens the door for you to 'stun-and-run'. The S.P.E.A.R tactic nails the guy as he moves in; it creates the time and space to strike back. If someone throws a punch at you in a crowded bar, you won't be able to jump back into a stance, block the punch and then counter attack, but you will flinch and if you strike from the flinch using the S.P.E.A.R. then that's good for you. The flinch is faster than anything else you can think of and it will get you tactically ready to terminate (as Steve would say).

R
E
A
C
T

Be aware that going to a strange house to ask for help could be potentially dangerous 《 **REACT** REMINDER

Now let's review some of the system's key points. The ideal S.P.E.A.R. tactic is to use the forearms. Remember the diamond shape? It's actually the shape of a spear's tip! This is more natural because of our instinct to cover our head by raising our arms. The tactical S.P.E.A.R. demands that we move forward towards the bad guy to engage the threat. The movement is like an impaling tool. It's not a block like using a real spear. You thrust it forwards for the attack. Although behaviourally we all want to move away from danger, tactically we need to move towards it. The S.P.E.A.R. as a visual icon will help you accomplish that action. The tactical S.P.E.A.R. will intercept the attack and inflict some pain. The pain will cause doubt and some hesitation on the attacker's part. That will give you the chance to move in with a counter or indeed run away.

The beauty of the S.P.E.A.R. is that it is tactical and protective at the same time. If you are surprised by an attack you flinch – convert, make contact and defend. The serendipity is that the flinch converted into a SPEAR often strikes vulnerable points on the bad guy even though you weren't trying to hit them.

The S.P.E.A.R. will protect you in a moment of ambush. The faster the attack, the faster the flinch and the faster you can defend yourself. You can use your survival system to spontaneously protect yourself and use that natural flinch to accelerate your response. Remember, you are already a survival machine. Embrace this and combine it with Steve's REACT principles and you will walk with more confidence.

That then is the S.P.E.A.R. Let's see how it fits into **REACT**. Tony uses the word 'tactical' and to go tactical is the same as to terminate, to finish it, take the initiative, stop the action and go home! That has to be the ultimate aim: to extract yourself from danger with as little fuss as possible, hopefully leaving the other guy wishing he'd stayed in bed that day!

R
E
A
C
T

REACT
REMINDER 》》 If your house is broken into at night, lock yourself in your bedroom. Call for help on a mobile or cellular phone so you can't be cut off

The S.P.E.A.R. (Spontaneous Protection Enabling Accelerated Response)

The verbal assault

The physical attack

The Flinch

Keep moving away and you will be hit

Convert the flinch into the S.P.E.A.R. and strike your attacker pre-emptively

**R
E
A
C
T**

NEAREST TARGET, NEAREST WEAPON

If we are agreed that Tony's S.P.E.A.R. system is a totally natural defensive mechanism which instantly creates a situation that we can take advantage of, what next? Where do we go from here? Nearest target, nearest weapon. You will have read this phrase earlier in the book and basically all it means is that whatever position you are in, in relationship to your assailant, there will be a body target staring you in the face. This being the case that target will be accessible to one or more of your natural weapons. So what do you do? That's right! Hit it! Grab it, kick it, bite it, pinch it, tear it as hard as you can! It doesn't matter what it is, just go for it! His eyes, ears, neck, fingers, balls – even his big toe – if that's your nearest target, get a grip! That way you don't have to waste time thinking about what target to go for, just hit the nearest thing to you with your most convenient weapon.

By using this principle you cut out the possibility of telegraphing your intention and you also eliminate the problem and tactical dilemma of 'What next?' Being encumbered with too many choices will slow you down. No matter what position you are in, your natural weapons are at your disposal. Believe me, the target will be there and it is quite probable that it will be the last place your attacker is expecting to be hit. The principle of nearest target, nearest weapon used as your pre-emptive strike will always get through. But remember, don't rely on just one strike. You must think in terms of a continuous and multiple attack – one, two, three!

USING YOUR BODY'S WEAPONS

Nearest target, nearest weapon is a good, sound concept. If it's in front of you, hit it, but just how do you do that and make it effective? At the risk of boring you, I say again 'ineffective self-defence is worse than no self-defence'. Your natural weapons are

REACT REMINDER >> Carry a 'dummy' purse or wallet with a little money and extinct credit cards in it to give to a thief if necessary. No mugger stops to check how much money he has stole from you

always available to you, so let's look at how best to use them.

Rule number one: never, ever, ever punch with a clenched fist. Why? Because it will hurt you. Not only will it hurt, it will hurt a lot and it will probably hurt you more than the person you have punched in the first place. Sprained, dislocated or broken fingers or even a fractured wrist is not a good way to start defending yourself. One thing's for sure, whoever is attacking you is not going to stop just because your hand hurts. Professional boxers don't tape up their hands and wear big gloves just to protect their opponent's good looks. Always think in terms of open hands. Slaps, rakes and fingers jabs are much more effective and versatile than punches, and if you must clench your fist, use the side of your hand like a hammer. Now let's look specifically at some of our body's weapons and how to use them.

Fingers

Strike to eye

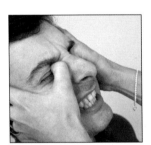
Thumb gouge to eyes

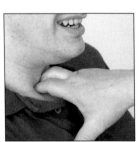
Strike to jugular notch

Open Hand

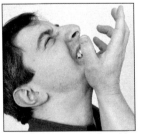
Heel palm strike under chin

Outside edge of hand to cervical vertebra

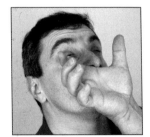
Inside edge of hand to infra orbital

Carry a bag with a short strap under your arm like you would carry a football and with your arm through the strap   **REACT REMINDER**

Cupped hand strike to ears

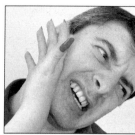

Backhand slap

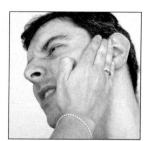

Slap to face

Raking face with finger nails

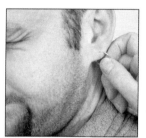

Tearing out earrings

Pulling hair

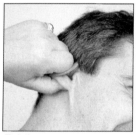

Twisting ears

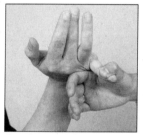

Bending back fingers

Gripping genitalia

Closed Hand

Hammer fist to lumbar vertebrae

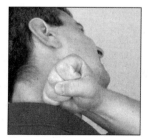

Hammer fist to brachial plexus

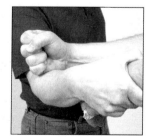

Hammer fist to radial nerve

R E A C T

REACT REMINDER »

If you walk past a street light at night check your shadow on the ground to see if you are being followed

Elbows

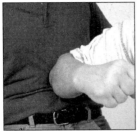
Strike to solar plexus

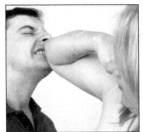
Strike to infra orbital

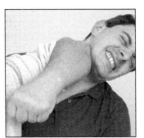
Strike to brachial plexus

Forearms

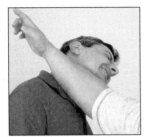
Forearm strike to brachial plexus

Forearm strike to infra orbital

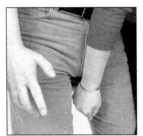
Forearm strike to groin

Head

Front head-butt to nose

Side head-butt to nose

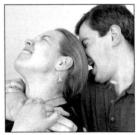
Rear head-butt to nose

Teeth

Biting the earlobe

Biting web of hand

Biting forearm

Don't carry all your money in one place

REACT REMINDER

REACT

Knees

Strike to the genitals

Strike to peroneal nerve

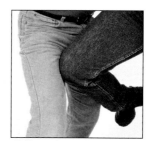
Strike to femoral nerve

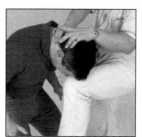
Strike to face

Strike to solar plexus

Knee drop to kidneys

Feet

Kick to genitals

Kick to knee joint (outside)

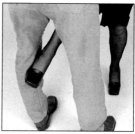
Kick to knee joint (inside)

Kick to shin

Stamp to ankle

Stamp to instep

REACT
REMINDER >> Always try to appear purposeful and confident.
Don't look like a victim

Forty-two photographs graphically depicting ways to inflict pain and damage to your attacker. Mark them well. But do not fall into the trap of thinking that one shot will do the trick. If one powerful, well-placed blow sends your assailant into the middle of next week, that's fantastic. Unfortunately, the chances of that are remote.

Seldom will a single blow floor a determined attacker.

You must always think in terms of multiple strikes (no less than three) and a continuous attack. However, it is essential that you try to make your first strike the most effective. You must have 200 percent commitment, you must explode into action and be totally focused. This first strike must, at the very least, line your assailant up for the second strike, which by the nature of the situation and the stress you are under, will probably not be as accurate or as powerful as the first. The placement of your second strike will be determined by where your opponent ends up after the first. This, of course, means you might miss altogether. In fact, your third strike could be the one that causes the most damage. If not, start again. It is crucial that you follow through and continue your attack, one, two, three, one, two, three and so on, even if your opponent is on the ground. Don't assume that because they're down they won't get up again. You must maintain a continuous attack with a second, third, fourth strike or whatever it takes. Your assailant must be totally subdued with controlled aggression. Remember, nearest weapon nearest target. Wherever your opponent is there will be targets in direct line with your natural weapons. Do not be defensive. Attack the attacker. Don't stop until the job is done and you or your loved ones are safe.

▶▶ **YOUR BODY'S NATURAL WEAPONS ARE ALWAYS WITH YOU.**

Unlike other weapons, they can't be taken away and used against you. You don't have to look for them or root around in your handbag or pocket. Let's look at how to use our natural weapons properly.

Never hide spare keys to your home outside - you could be seen retrieving them ⟨⟨ **REACT** REMINDER

R
E
A
C
T

HOW TO USE YOUR HANDS

Lashing out is ineffective. You will probably break your hand and antagonise your attacker which will result in additional injury to yourself. For any strike to be effective it should have four ingredients: speed, power, accuracy and surprise. Of these speed and surprise are the most important. Fast, not necessarily hard, can do the trick. The velocity of your strike is the key to its power; you do not need great strength to achieve a knockout. Make no mistake, you must strike as hard as you can, but it is the speed that will do the damage. Think of a bullet fired from a gun, a tiny piece of lead that will tear you apart, destroy internal organs and probably kill you. And why? Because it is travelling faster than the speed of sound. Speed is the key to using your hands as a weapon.

Fingers Only used on soft targets, the fingers should be used to thrust, rake, tear, pinch, grip and squeeze. Finger strikes to the eyes have to be performed with conviction. The hand should be locked into a semi-curved claw and shot directly into the attacker's eye sockets with a gouging and tearing action, or raked across the eyes with a flick of the wrist. If pulling the hair, either on the head or the pubic region, grip as close to the root as possible and pull with a snapping action. When gripping the penis or the testicles, lock on, twist and pull in one powerful action.

Slap A hard, fast slap to the side of the face can sometimes have a more powerful psychological effect than a punch. This strike can be performed with the palm or the back of the hand. A cupped slap hand directed against the ears causes a pocket of air to be compressed into the ear and can result in a burst eardrum.

REACT REMINDER Carry a high visibility vest in your car. If you break down, wearing it will make you look less like a driver in distress and more like an official

Hammer fist   This is a closed hand-clubbing blow using the bottom of the fist. It is a powerful technique that can be used to break a grip or strike vulnerable body targets. It is unlikely that you will damage your hand using this blow.

Palm heel   A very simple and effective open hand strike. The heel of the hand must be powerfully driven upwards under the nose or chin. This will snap the head back and leave the assailant open for follow up attacks to the throat, solar plexus or groin.

Knife hand   The classic karate blow delivered with the edge of the hand. The striking area is the fleshy part between the base of the little finger and the wrist. It is imperative that the hand is ridged, slightly bent and the little finger is kept tight against the other fingers with the thumb tucked in. This weapon is ideal for attacking the side or the back of the neck.

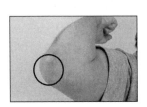

Elbows   The elbow is one of your most effective weapon if being attacked from the rear. The point of the elbow is solid and very effective against the nose, throat, solar plexus and kidneys. Although the elbow is a very solid and powerful weapon it is also a fairly fragile joint and doesn't stand up well to too much abuse. Therefore, try to use it to attack soft targets only. The forearm smash could be considered a sort of an elbow strike, but it is best utilised, and very effective, against an attacker who is very close and directly in front of you.

Web hand   By spreading the thumb and index finger, you will tighten the web of the hand. With the palm uppermost the hand is driven horizontally under the nose or into the throat.

R
E
A
C
T

HOW TO USE YOUR FEET

As with your hands, lashing out with your feet is ineffective and you will probably end up flat on your back. The essentials of kicking are stability, focus and recovery. Flashy martial arts high kicks do not work and have no place on the street! You should never even consider trying to kick anyone above the groin. The higher you kick the more unstable you are and when one of those kicks to the head fails, not only will you feel stupid, you will probably be feeling stupid from a hospital bed. Keep your kicks low, certainly no higher than the groin and preferably directed towards the knee, shin or ankle. Knowing how to kick is an essential part of your arsenal, therefore you must be aware of recovery. This means kicking and getting your foot back from the action without your opponent grabbing it or you losing your balance and falling over. The higher you try to kick, the harder this is to achieve. Although not strictly a kick, I have included blows with the knees into this section. A knee strike to the groin is the one most people are familiar with.

Front kick A front kick can be delivered in two ways. First, the knee is lifted and the foot is shot out in a straight line, hitting its target with either the ball of the foot, the toe or the heel. The second is a rising kick, where the foot rises in an arc, rather like kicking a football, and lands with the instep in a slapping action between your opponent's legs. This can be an easy kick to defend against so it must be executed with speed, surprise and focus.

Side kick Usually delivered to the side or back of the knee joint, the sidekick is executed by lifting the knee and thrusting the leg out in a sideways, piston-like action. It utilises the outer edge of the hard soles of your boots or shoes. If your attacker is on the ground a sidekick to the head will keep them there.

REACT REMINDER >> Be careful if a van with sliding doors parks next to you, particularly if the car park is deserted

Stomping kick If grabbed from behind, a stomping kick with all your force, using the heel of your boot on your attacker's instep, will aid your escape. The other use for this kick is when your attacker is already down when a powerful stomping kick to the knee or ankle will keep them down.

Knee strike Knee strikes are a solid and effective close-quarter weapon. Hold on to your opponent, keep him close and drive your knees hard into his legs and groin. If possible, hold onto his head or hair, snap it downwards and deliver a powerful rising knee strike to the nose and teeth.

TEETH

Biting may seem a little unsavoury to say the least, but if you are fighting for survival and biting becomes your only option to escape then do it. Don't think about it, just do it! However, we're not merely talking about doing it just hard enough to make someone yell, or more to the point, to make them feel really pissed off with you and therefore even more dangerous. No, we're talking about causing enough damage and pain to disable your attacker. So, if you have made the decision to bite, take a piece of flesh, not too big, from a fatty area such as the ear lobe, inner arm, inner thigh, etc., whatever is nearest. Clamp on tight and shake your head like a dog. Rip and tear the flesh off in a bite-size lump. Never plan to bite, that's a good way to lose your teeth. But if you need to bite to save yourself, then do it hard. Biting is done to cause intensive pain and trauma, and you are likely to draw blood. Also, human bites often become infected because of the saliva. Tough luck on him. However, the downside to biting is the risk of contracting the AIDS virus, but given the choice of biting to stay alive or the million-to-one chance of catching something nasty, then bite for all your worth.

R
E
A
C
T

To avoid a gang on the street use other pedestrians to shield you as you pass

REACT
REMINDER

CHOKES AND STRANGLES

Neck-locks are potentially killing techniques. They fall into two categories, the choke and the strangle. The choke cuts off the air

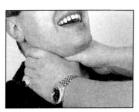

Choke

supply to the brain by exerting pressure on the throat and larynx. Choking is a slow and painful journey to unconsciousness or even death. It can take a minute or more for a choke to work and even if death doesn't occur serious damage to the throat is common. If you had choked a person to death while defending yourself against them, it would be particularly difficult to justify in a court of law. The strangle, on the other hand, applies pressure to both the

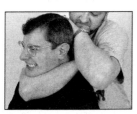

Strangle

jugular vein and carotid artery, cutting off the blood supply and oxygen to the brain. Quick and relatively painless, it is possible to render a person unconscious in less than 15 seconds if continuous pressure applied. If you release the strangle as soon as your attacker becomes unconsciousness, a full recovery will be made in a few seconds. However, a carotid restraint is potentially deadly if held on too long, and is guaranteed to be lethal if held for two minutes or more. In self-defence terms two minutes is a lifetime.

EYES AND VOICE

Your eyes and voice are among your most powerful physical and psychological weapon. In fact, your voice could easily be considered the principle weapon in your physical arsenal. Used correctly it has more impact than any kick or punch. Confident or aggressive dialogue delivered in a firm, low, steady tone coupled with piercing and aggressive eye contact can psyche an opponent out. It may even paralyse a person to the spot just long enough for you to act. Strong eye contact can also keep a person at bay. In fact, if you want to get someone closer you won't do it with intense eye contact. With a combination of your voice and eyes you can finish a potential confrontation before it starts. We have all heard the

R
E
A
C
T

REACT REMINDER ▶▶▶ Never load yourself down with so much shopping that you do not have a free hand

expression, 'If looks could kill, I'd be dead by now.' Another way of using your eyes is to avert your gaze for a moment, in order to make your assailant think you are frightened, which could line him up for a pre-emptive strike.

The yell. We have all seen and heard the martial artists who scream like wild animals when they attack. You may imagine this is a shout of rage or hatred, but no, the trained martial artists can produce a blood curling yell or *kiai* with a totally rational and calm mind. This shout can force a whole room full of people to involuntarily step back and freeze. The *kiai*, directed against a single opponent at close quarters can be absolutely devastating. However, it's not just a very loud shout, it must have focus and emotional content to work.

Focus your indignation

Avoid staying at a party if you are the only female, you could be putting yourself at risk

REACT
REMINDER

R
E
A
C
T

BODY TARGETS

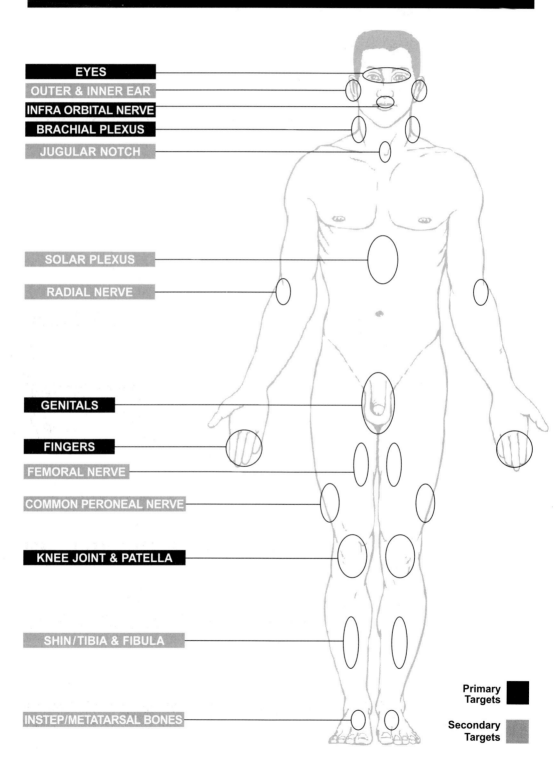

EYES

OUTER & INNER EAR

INFRA ORBITAL NERVE

BRACHIAL PLEXUS

JUGULAR NOTCH

SOLAR PLEXUS

RADIAL NERVE

GENITALS

FINGERS

FEMORAL NERVE

COMMON PERONEAL NERVE

KNEE JOINT & PATELLA

SHIN/TIBIA & FIBULA

INSTEP/METATARSAL BONES

Primary Targets

Secondary Targets

R
E
A
C
T

BODY TARGETS

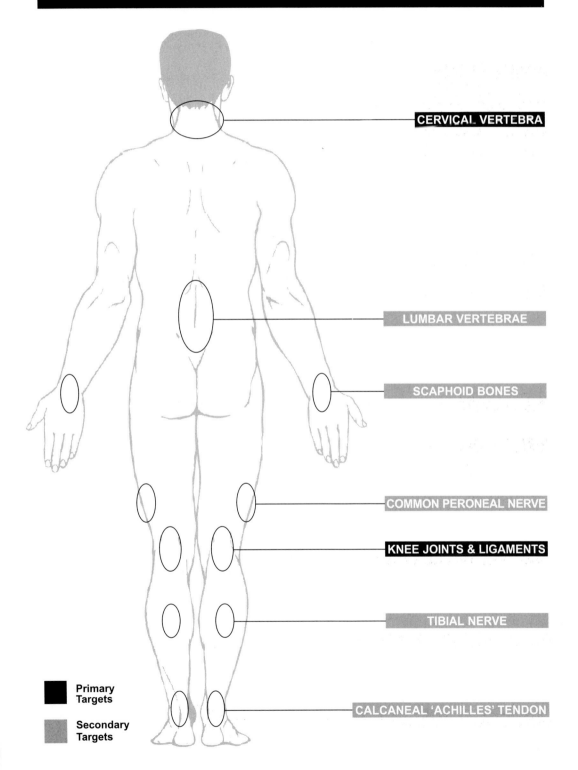

CERVICAL VERTEBRA

LUMBAR VERTEBRAE

SCAPHOID BONES

COMMON PERONEAL NERVE

KNEE JOINTS & LIGAMENTS

TIBIAL NERVE

CALCANEAL 'ACHILLES' TENDON

Primary Targets

Secondary Targets

REACT

BODY TARGETS

While there are literary hundreds of body targets, I have highlighted only 19 because in my opinion attacking these targets will give you the most effective results. However, of all these targets six of them should be considered primary. They are the eyes, neck, nose, groin, fingers and knees. Blows to these primary targets will not only cause pain, but also injury. Research has shown that, in the event of a vicious attack such as rape, attempting to defend yourself with blows that only hurt the attacker can result in just making them angry, even more aggressive and possibly more intent on causing you further harm to the extent of even killing you for having had the audacity to try and defend yourself.

INEFFECTIVE SELF-DEFENCE IS WORSE THAN NO SELF-DEFENCE.

Most people who commit acts of violence are nasty, hostile, aggressive excuses for humanity, who think only of themselves. When faced with ineffectual or half-hearted aggression towards them, they become even more confident, and will explode with even more violence towards you when, in fact, you are the one that should be exploding! Exploding into action, totally focused mentally and physically on doing whatever's necessary to take this person out. Strike those body targets hard and fast, but always remember: nearest target, nearest weapon.

Never, ever strike only once. Think in terms of at least three times, in quick succession. If necessary, keep on going until the job is done.

EYES

Probably the most vulnerable of all body targets. A powerful finger strike or gouge will result in immediate and debilitating pain in one, possibly both eyes followed by shock and trauma. Uncontrollable watering, blurred vision, almost certainly temporary blindness and

REACT REMINDER If you think you are being stalked notify the police immediately, don't try to deal with it yourself

probably permanent blindness will be caused if the eye bulb is ruptured. Sharp fingernails can tear the eyelids and surrounding tissue, which can cause infection and compilations.

Bearing in mind the severity of the injuries you can cause, a strike to the eyes should only be executed when you consider it absolutely necessary. Although the thought of blinding someone may seem shocking, an attacker may be strangling the life out of you and if you do not escape you are likely to die, so do it. You cannot afford to hesitate. Do it. Take an eye.

EARS

A twisting or tearing action on the external part of the ear will result in extreme pain. If an attacker is wearing earrings which pierce the ear, grip the earring between the finger and thumb and with a fast snapping action, tear it through the flesh. This will cause excruciating pain, shock and trauma. Biting the ear is also extremely effective. For the most positive and painful results take only a small piece of flesh and nip it between your front teeth. A cupped hand palm strike to both sides of the head will cause a double percussive shock wave which can result in ruptured ear drums, unconsciousness or concussion. There will be extreme pain shock and trauma.

INFRA ORBITAL NERVE (base of nose)

Even a light blow to the base of the nose will cause extreme pain, extensive watering of the eyes and nausea. A more powerful blow and the top lip will be split and front teeth could be chipped or even dislodged. A very heavy blow will almost certainly result in a nosebleed, trauma and possibly unconsciousness. The infra orbital nerve may sound like a very specific point of aim, and to an extent this is true, but I bet you can remember the last time you were hit on the nose, even accidentally. For a split second you thought you were going to die, didn't you? It's that split second that lines your attacker up for the second and third strikes, which could just save your life.

R
E
A
C
T

Always leave enough space between you and the car in front to enable you to drive round that vehicle should you need to make a quick getaway

REACT
REMINDER

BRACHIAL PLEXUS NERVES (side of neck)

These are the nerve fibres emanating from the vertebrae in the side of the neck. A heavy blow to this area will cause intense pain, numbing of the arm and hand and possible low-level unconsciousness. A slightly lower and much more powerful blow could fracture the collarbone. A common side-effect of a broken collarbone is pinching or even laceration of the brachial plexus nerves. This will cause instant paralysis of the arm, shock, trauma and nausea.

JUGULAR NOTCH

Hard pressure with the finger tips in a downward and inward direction of about 45 degrees will cause pain and shock to the system. Although this is not a disabling blow it can serve as a method of distraction to precede another strike. It will also stop an attacker's forward movement, as there is an involuntary reflex action to move away from the pressure. Hard pressure will also throw an attacker off balance to the rear, possibly causing them to fall over in a backward direction.

SOLAR PLEXUS

A powerful elbow strike to the centre of the solar plexus will produce a shock wave. This will result in contraction of the diaphragm and spasm of the intercostal rib muscles. Normal movement of the diaphragm will cease and result in respiratory paralysis. Breathing will stop for a few moments. Even a light blow can have this effect, but a deep penetrating blow can cause shock, nausea, vomiting and even unconsciousness.

RADIAL NERVE

A powerful strike to the radial nerve area, which is located just below the elbow joint at the top of the muscle on the outside edge of the forearm, will cause intense pain and temporary paralysis of the arm and possibly the hand. An involuntary flexing of the fingers

REACT REMINDER If you witness a violent incident or crime on the street don't try to help. Put a safe distance between you and the incident and telephone the police

sometimes occurs, possibly releasing the grip on a weapon, etc.

GENITALS

Kicks, knee or hand strikes to the groin in both sexes will cause intense pain and possibly shock, nausea, vomiting and even unconsciousness. The percussive shock of a solid blow could rupture the bladder, resulting in the complication of blood and urine leaking into the abdominal cavity. With a powerful kick it is possible to fracture the pubic bone, resulting in a total inability to walk or even stand.

Male The penis can be attacked with a blow or a grip. This will cause moderate pain and discomfort but the most common form of damage is bruising. Although extremely painful and debilitating, serious damage from a blow to the testicles is unusual. This is because they are extremely mobile within the scrotum and therefore difficult to trap. Nevertheless, sudden pressure from a tight grip and squeeze with the hand will result in excruciating pain, shock, loss of breath, even vomiting and possible unconsciousness. Remember, all men are acutely aware of their vulnerability in this area, therefore never let an assailant suspect that his groin is going to be your target.

Female A kick or knee strike to the vulva, the external female sex organ, will cause intense pain, shock, loss of breath and nausea. Due to the loose tissue of the labia, the inner and outer lips at the vaginal entrance, the most common form of damage is excessive swelling and bruising.

A kick directed to the underside, towards the back of the female genital region, can result in severe lacerations and the bursting of the back end of the vulva. It is also likely this will tear the perineum, the fibrous tissue and muscles between the vaginal canal and the anus. Intense pain, shock, trauma, nausea, vomiting and possible unconsciousness can all occur.

R
E
A
C
T

Keep the bushes and shrubs in your garden well trimmed to reduce the availability of hiding places for criminals

FINGERS

Fracturing the metacarpals or dislocating the bones in the fingers is comparatively easy. The fifth metacarpal, or little finger, is the easiest of all. The joints of the second, third and fourth can be dislocated by bending them backwards at the joint. These dislocations can be compounded by pushing the head of the bone through the flesh. Intense pain, shock, nausea and an inability to use the hand will result.

FEMORAL NERVE

This nerve lies approximately halfway between the groin and knee, along the centre line of the inner thigh. A powerful knee strike will result in intense pain, shock, nausea and a temporary immobilisation of the leg.

COMMON PERONEAL NERVE

This nerve lies just above the back of the knee, at the base of the outer thigh muscle. A powerful knee strike will result in intense pain, shock, nausea and total immobilisation of the leg. A strike to this nerve can be so effective that the opposite leg can sometimes be sympathetically affected. A deep penetrating strike to this spot will immobilise the largest of attackers.

KNEE JOINT

Kicks to the front, side and the back of the knee can cause tears and sprains to the muscles and ligaments. Probably the most effective knee strikes are directed to the sides of the knee joint, and the most painful injury is a torn cartilage which will rip the ligaments from their fixed position on the tibia and fibula, the two lower bones of the leg. Attacking the knee joints will cause intense pain, shock, nausea and possibly total immobilisation of the leg. It takes less than 40 pounds of pressure to dislocate a knee joint.

SHIN

Attacking the tibia or fibula, in the lower leg, with a powerful kick can fracture one, or even both bones. Nauseating pain and a total inability

REACT REMINDER >> Try to keep in good physical shape so you'll have a better chance of survival should something untoward happen

to put any weight on the limb will ensue. If the fracture is very severe and shattered bone tears blood vessels, a huge swelling of the lower limb will accrue. Shock, nausea and total immobilisation are almost certain.

INSTEP

A stomping kick onto the instep – that part of the foot between the ankle and the toes – can displace or fracture the metatarsal bones. Although very painful, it is not totally disabling and therefore should be used as a distraction to precede another strike or your escape. Standing and walking may still be possible, but pursuing a victim would not be an option.

ACHILLES TENDON

This is the large tendon that joins the calf muscles just above the heel. A powerful kick with the edge of the foot downward at a 45-degree angle can sprain, tear or rupture this tendon. If bones in the ankle were dislocated or fractured, this would be an extremely traumatic injury. Severe pain, extensive swelling, shock, nausea, vomiting and loss of consciousness are all possible. Walking on the injured foot would be almost an impossibility.

TIBIAL NERVE

This is the lower end of the sciatic nerve which runs down the back of the leg and through the calf muscle. A powerful kick to the top of the calf, just below the knee, will cause intense pain, shock, trauma and temporary immobilisation of the leg.

SCAPHOID BONES

The small bones in the back of the hand are easily damaged. The wrist is a complicated joint and a blow to these small bones can cause fractures that are difficult to treat and do not heal easily. Forcibly bending the wrist backwards or forwards can fracture or dislocate the bones causing extreme pain, shock and trauma. Swelling of the wrist and an inability to move the fingers is also common.

R
E
A
C
T

Before getting into your car always check to make sure there's no-one hiding inside it **》REACT REMINDER**

LUMBAR VERTEBRAE

An elbow strike or kick to the lower lumbar region can have a catastrophic effect on an attacker. Dynamic pressure to the spinal cord may produce partial to complete paralysis. An intense muscle spasm can break the bones or dislodge a disc and if a vertebra is crushed or a disc has created direct pressure to the spinal cord, paralysis of the body below the point of impact can occur.

CERVICAL VERTEBRA

Spinal cord shock or whiplash is the minimum possible damage resulting from a powerful blow to the back of the neck. However, a severed spinal cord, commonly referred to as a broken neck, will result in total paralysis from the point of impact downwards. If the cord is severed above the fifth cervical vertebra, acute respiratory arrest will accrue and death can be almost instantaneous. In fact, a common saying in the medical world is 'Cervical vertebra 3, 4, and 5 keep the diaphragm alive.' A blow to the cervical vertebrae should only be considered if your believe your life to be in grave danger.

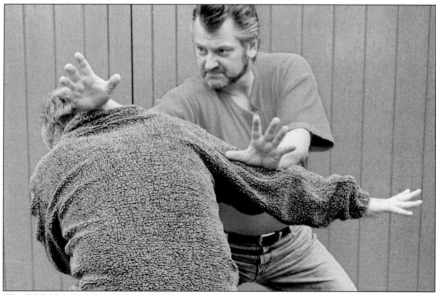

The SPEAR will strike vital targets without trying

REACT **REMINDER** >>> If you are woken in the night by burglars in your home, don't charge blindly downstairs. You will be putting yourself in more danger by confronting an unknown situation

SOME LITTLE TRICKS

Basically, this is stuff that works! Nothing fancy, nothing complicated or hard to remember. A handful of little tricks up your sleeve can make all the difference when your back's against the wall. We've looked at your natural weapons, we've looked at the vulnerable target areas of the body and how to attack them, but let's take a closer look at some ways of making your defensive response more effective. As with many things in life it's often the simplest that work the best, and the best thing you can do to an attacker (that's the best thing for you, not him!) is to inflict instant and intense pain. Not just the 'ouch, that hurt' type of pain but the kind that will sicken him, make him want to throw up and make him wish he was somewhere else. Remember, the only pain this type recognise is their own.

There are many unprotected areas of your attacker's body that can be hurt very quickly and easily. Attacking some of these areas may effect a release that enables you to escape, or create an opening for another defensive strike. Obvious things like pulling the hair can be very effective. However, many people can resist the pulling of hairs on the top of the head, but the short ones at the back or nape of the neck near to the hairline are another story. If these hairs are pulled in an upwards direction towards the top of the head, the pain is intense. Not many people will withstand it and will want to break away as fast as they can.

The pinch is one of your best weapons.

The forefinger and thumb, or better still, the thumb and a hard object such as a pen, can have almost the same effect as a pair of pliers. Twisting, grasping and tearing can all be achieved with the simple pinch. Applied with sufficient force to the lips, ear lobes, nose, Adam's apple, or indeed any fleshy part of the body, you will inflict immense pain. A powerful forefinger and thumb pinch to a testicle will crush it like a grape. Of all your fingers the thumb is

If you are home alone at night, wait until the morning before emptying rubbish into the dustbin

REACT
REMINDER

R
E
A
C
T

Don't underestimate the pinch

the most effective weapon. The tip of the thumb, especially with a sharp nail, pushed hard into the bone on the top or bottom of the eye socket will cause immediate and excruciating pain. A direct eye gouge with one or both thumbs is obvious, but for the most effective results use the thumb against the inside of the eye sockets with the force exerted towards the outside of the head. Hooking the thumbs into the corners of the mouth or the nostrils will result in an almost instant release, and ramming both thumbs into the nerve centres which lie at the hinge of the jaw in the recesses under the ear will cause extreme pain. Direct pressure of the thumb into the infra orbital nerve at the base of the nose will also inflict immense pain on your attacker. Hook your fingers around the jaw bone, pull with your fingers and push with your thumb. Try it on yourself; it hurts, doesn't it?

A strong grip is good if you have one, but if your grip is not that strong, don't worry. Knowing where to get hold is the trick. The soft sides of the waistline just below the rib cage, or 'love handles' as some might call them, don't require a strong grip to bring tears to someone's eyes. Hold both sides if you can and squeeze with all your might. This can cause massive shock and trauma to the system. The fleshy part of the back of the arm under the biceps, inside the thigh and the ridge of fat and sinew that runs from under the arm to the nipple are all very susceptible to a powerful gripping action and will result in extreme pain. There is also, of course, the excruciating agony you can cause by gripping and squeezing the testicles. None of this stuff requires pinpoint accuracy. Don't confuse it with the arts of nerve-striking which requires the skill and knowledge of an

REACT REMINDER >> If using the Underground, avoid unmanned stations at night and don't wait on deserted platforms

acupuncturist. Also, don't think of attacking any of these places in advance – think of 'nearest target, nearest weapon'. If it's there, grab it. Believe me, you will not have time to go looking for these targets.

There are no wrist locks or arm locks in this book, not because I don't like them but because they take too long to learn and most of them won't work for you when faced with the wild melee of a street attack. Another fundamental fault is that the vast majority of self-defence instructors who teach this sort of technique, for some reason, omit to tell their students that in the original combat systems designed for the battlefield none of these locks and restraints would be even attempted unless preceded with powerful blows to anatomical weak points – usually the eyes. In fact, some of these strikes have cute little names like 'the blinder' or 'smashing

Painful but impractical

the eyes'. The point is that even back then they knew that a fancy wrist lock wasn't going to work without some method of distracting the other guy's attention. So, if it's unlikely that you are going to break your attacker's arm or wrist, what can you break? Fingers! Little pinkies will break like pencils! You don't need to be strong to grab a finger and snap it! The little finger is the best but any of them will do. Roll the finger back against the joint and as you feel it give way, shake it like a dog with a bone. It will make your attacker think very carefully about continuing the assault.

None of this needs any great skill. But don't think of these little tricks as the mainstay of your self-defence arsenal; rather think of them as quick and simple methods of inflicting some serious pain on your attacker. Use them to create an opening.

REACT

Pinching

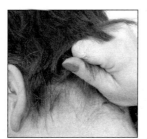

Pull upwards from the nape of the neck

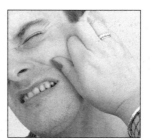

Squeeze and twist

Pinch and pull

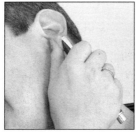

Grip with pen or similar object and tear downwards

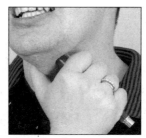

Try and make your thumb and the pen meet behind the windpipe

Grip and twist

Hooking

Hook thumb nail under eye socket

Push thumbs into corner of eye sockets and exert force to the outside of the head

Hook thumb into the mouth or nostril and tear with a downward movement

Gripping

Direct pressure to the small indentation behind the ears

Direct pressure to the infra orbital nerve under the nose

Squeeze with a twisting motion

**R
E
A
C
T**

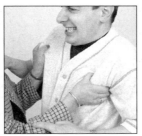

Squeeze and twist

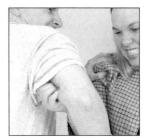

Try and make fingers and thumb meet behind the sinew

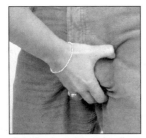

Grip firmly, digging in the nails and pull towards the elbow

Grip firmly, twist and pull

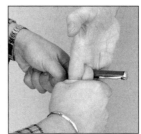

Grip firmly, digging in the nails and squeeze tightly

Insert pen or similar object between finger joints and squeeze hard

Finger breaks

Break or dislocate bone and shake vigorously

Break or dislocate bone and shake vigorously

Break finger and dislocate thumb

Break or dislocate bone and shake vigorously

Break or dislocate bone and shake vigorously

Force fingers apart to tear web between fingers

R
E
A
C
T

4 THINGS TO BEAR IN MIND

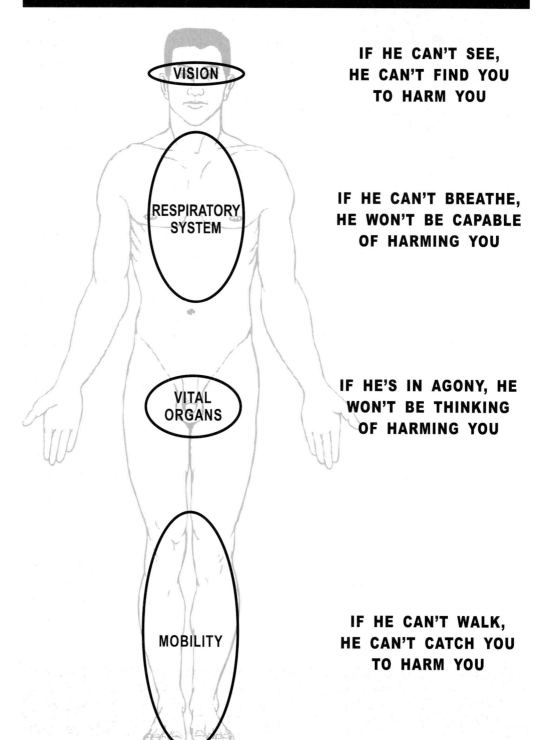

VISION

RESPIRATORY
SYSTEM

VITAL
ORGANS

MOBILITY

IF HE CAN'T SEE,
HE CAN'T FIND YOU
TO HARM YOU

IF HE CAN'T BREATHE,
HE WON'T BE CAPABLE
OF HARMING YOU

IF HE'S IN AGONY, HE
WON'T BE THINKING
OF HARMING YOU

IF HE CAN'T WALK,
HE CAN'T CATCH YOU
TO HARM YOU

R
E
A
C
T

YOUR MORAL DILEMMA

What do you do now?

What dilemma? This piece of scum has just invaded your life and, as a result of picking on the wrong person, is now feeling pretty sick. Why should you have a moral dilemma? 'Serves him right,' you might say and that's fine if that's what your instincts tell you. However, remember you're supposed to be one of the good guys. The law is quite clear: you have the right to defend yourself with 'reasonable force' and, as far as you're concerned, that's exactly what you have done. You can now get away, run as fast as you can and report the incident to the authorities, leaving him to his own devices. It's his problem now. Your moral dilemma, however, is that if you have totally disabled your assailant so that he is of no further danger to you whatsoever, but in doing so have endangered his life, what are you going to do now? Don't get me wrong, I'm not trying to frighten you off. You must defend yourself. If you think you are in danger, you owe it to yourself, your family and friends to defend yourself. So this is not a question of 'should I or shouldn't I?' You should! But split lips and black eyes are one thing, leaving someone choking on his own blood and vomit is something else.

REACT should have empowered you and given you the confidence to believe in your ability to protect yourself, to give yourself permission to take control of a situation and terminate the threat. However, terminate does not mean 'leave him for dead'. If you have inflicted sufficient pain or damage to extract yourself and leave the other guy licking his wounds, that's OK. If the damage you have caused him could result in his death, even if he was trying to kill you, you are morally and legally obliged to attend to him and not leave the scene. Once again, only you will know on the day. That's why it's a dilemma. I can't tell you what to do, no-one can, but these are the guidelines:

If you disturb a burglar in your home, never try to block his exit. Try to get a clear description of him and observe what, if anything, he touches for fingerprints later

REACT REMINDER

R E A C T

- *Always defend yourself, no question!*

- *Only defend yourself with what you consider to be 'reasonable force' under the circumstances.*

- *Get away if you can.*

- *Always report the incident to the authorities.*

- *Your moral dilemma: if you have inflicted serious damage that could endanger life, call an ambulance and, if you can bring yourself to do it, assist your assailant. It's not an easy one, but it's something you must think about!*

REACT is not a book on first aid. However, I would recommend to all the readers of **REACT** that you acquire a knowledge of rudimentary procedures. The Collins Gem *First Aid* is an excellent pocket-sized handbook, full of information on how to handle emergency situations.

The first-aid considerations as far as self-defence is concerned are based on the following three factors:

AIRWAY ▪ BREATHING ▪ CIRCULATION

ABC is the basis for providing vital life-saving treatment to a person you may have justifiably injured as a result of your defensive tactics. The ABC formula will have maximum results with minimum treatment.

AIRWAY

The airway consists of the mouth, nasal passages and the throat. If the airway becomes blocked, the person will die.

Likely causes of airway obstruction

- *Mucus, blood or vomit in the throat.*

- *Broken or dislodged teeth.*

- *Crushing of the windpipe as the result of a blow.*

- *Swelling of the lining of the airway as a result of a blow or constriction.*

REACT REMINDER >> If you break down and have to park at the side of the road, turn your wheels away from the traffic, that way if your vehicle is clipped from behind it will push your car away from danger

Treatment

This mainly consists of cleaning the airway of any obstructions and can be achieved by:

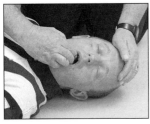

Clear the airway

- *Sweeping out any obstruction with the fingers or any other suitable implement.*

- *Tilting the head back and lifting the chin upwards can sometimes clear a blockage.*

- *Slapping the back between the shoulder blades can help to dislodge obstructions.*

- *Applying pressure to the abdomen in a position mid-way between the tip of the breast bone and the navel (Heimlich manoeuvre).*

- *Placing the person on their side in the recovery position, this will allow blood and mucus to freely drain away.*

Kneel next to him, bring the arm furthest from you across his chest

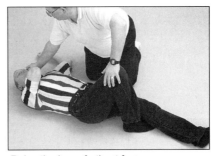

Raise the knee furthest from you

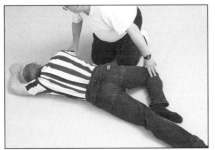

Gently pull on the knee turning him towards you, make sure his knee remains at right angles to his body

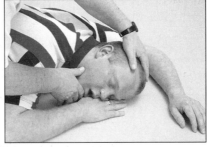

Gently push the head back to ensure a clear airway and check his breathing

Be constantly aware of your surroundings when parked in drive-ins and always be ready to leave quickly .

REACT REMINDER

R E A C T

Bear in mind that the mouth is the dirtiest place on the human body. It is moist, warm and full of bacteria. The risk of blood-to-blood contact and blood-to-saliva contact is high so try to avoid both. If you think you have been contaminated, wash the area immediately with soap and hot water and seek medical aid.

BREATHING

Check to see if the person is still breathing (more than an occasional gasp is required before breathing would be considered normal).

- *Look for movement in the chest.*
- *Listen for any breath sounds.*
- *Feel for exhaled breath against your face.*
- *This should be done all at once and for about ten seconds.*

Treatment

- *If the person's airway is blocked it will need clearing.*
- *If breathing is absent you may consider applying cardio-pulmonary resuscitation (CPR), but remember the dangers of contamination from blood and saliva during mouth-to-mouth contact*

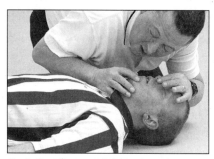 

Push the chin up and tilt the head back. Pinch the nose closed.   *Take a deep breath and blow strongly into the mouth. Watch for the chest to rise.*

- *Place the person on their side in the recovery position*

CIRCULATION

Most adults have five to six litres of blood in their body and this travels

REACT REMINDER >> If you have a lift home at night from a friend or a taxi ask them to wait until you are safely inside your home before leaving

around the system at a phenomenal speed. In most people all the blood will complete its journey around the body in less than one minute. This circulatory system is extremely vulnerable to damage, including visible and non-visible blood loss. Indeed, it is quite possible for a person to lose all the blood from their circulatory system and not spill one drop outside the body! Internal organs will bleed severely if damaged by a powerful blow. Once again it is quite simple – if a person loses too much blood, either inside or outside the body, they will die.

Treatment

As you would have no indication of internal bleeding, external blood loss can be our only consideration from an emergency first aid point of view.

- *All treatment of blood loss should be centred on plugging the hole or preventing the flow from wherever it is leaking. This may involve putting a suitable absorbent material over the wound. Anything that is relatively clean may be used as a dressing.*

- *Severe blood loss, particularly from blood vessels, i.e. arteries and veins, may require a different treatment. Blood loss from arteries is bright red and sprays out under high pressure. In this case you will need to apply very strong pressure around the area on the heart side of the wound. You will need to squeeze hard enough to stop the flow of blood through the artery and consequently stop the bleeding. Veins also bleed profusely, but the blood from veins is darker red and is under much lower pressure. The same principle used for treating blood loss from an artery can be applied to veins.*

Again, you must be aware of the dangers of blood-to-blood contact.

Whilst all this is going on, don't forget yourself. Check yourself carefully. If you have been involved in a highly physical confrontation you will have vast quantities of adrenaline coursing through your body and you may not be aware that you have received an injury or even a severe wound. If you have been injured, seek immediate medical attention.

R E A C T

Beware of people who contact you by telephone to research personal information   《《 **REACT** REMINDER

REACT >

R E A C T SURVIVAL FILE

Most of the topics covered in this section could easily become books in their own right. However, because each subject is so vast I have decided to treat them separately from the main text of the **REACT** system. Nevertheless, the principles of **REACT** still apply to all of the situations in this section.

The Survival File is an aid to your ability to recognise and evaluate given situations in order to take effective action. Throughout the book I have stressed being switched on to potential danger because spotting trouble in advance is your best means of avoiding it. Prevention is better than cure. This statement is as true for self-defence as it is for your health. Some common sense, a little foresight, the principles of **REACT** and you can avoid trouble.

The Survival File is your instant reference to understanding some fundamentals of violent behaviour. Why does it happen? What sort of people commit violent acts and why? The file will go some way to answering many of these questions and hopefully dispel some of the myths about certain elements of violent crime, such as rape and stalking. I have designed the pages of this section with quick, easy-to-follow bullet points and I make no apologies for repeating some of the information that has already appeared in the book. If the Survival File helps you to understand how and why some violence happens, you may just be able to avoid it.

Remember, it takes two to argue. Make sure you're not one of them.

RAPE

Contrary to popular belief, rape is not simply a sex crime but a violent crime revolving around domination and power over the victim. Sexual assaults vary from the quick grope on a crowded train to the full-blown violation of rape.

Rape can traumatise a victim for the rest of his or her life. Yes! Men can be raped as well as women. It may not be to the same extent, but the risk is there and just as traumatic. Rape comes with the distinct possibility of being beaten, mutilated or killed as well as becoming pregnant or contracting a sexually transmitted disease.

Most cases of rape are perpetrated by men who know their victims and are often planned well in advance. About 50 per cent of attacks take place in the victim's own home with many more in the rapist's home or hotel rooms. It is very difficult to accuse a person of rape if you were in his house or a hotel room with him.

Rape is an appalling crime against a person and there should be no half measures when dealing with it. A determined rapist has to be terminated with total commitment. You are going to be abused and you will have to live with that forever. Your aggression must overwhelm him. As I said before, you will probably know the person, you may just have spent a very enjoyable evening with him and now he thinks he is entitled to a reward. Shock tactics sometimes work: shout, scream, smash the furniture, throw a chair through the window, stick your fingers down your throat and make yourself vomit, evacuate your bladder or bowels. If it stops you being raped, it's worth it. Rape is not about sex. Although the definition of rape is the act of forced sexual intercourse involving the sexual organs of one person and the sexual organs, anus or mouth of another, quite often the rapist is sexually inadequate and unable to have sex in the normal way. Rape is really about power and domination. The rapist may happily use a bottle, screwdriver or chair leg to rape you. Sexual intercourse won't kill you, but a broken beer bottle probably will.

If you fight back there is a very good chance that you will avoid being raped. Submitting to rape in the hope of avoiding injury is no guarantee whatsoever that you will survive. However, feigning submission to create an opportunity to strike is another thing entirely.

- *Rape isn't 'just one of those things that happens'. Rape has a devastating, traumatic effect on its victims. Nearly a third of all rape victims will experience rape-related post-traumatic stress disorder.*

- *Over 70 per cent of all rape victims know their attacker.*

- *Women who dress provocatively are not 'asking for it'. Whatever your mode of dress, no-one deserves to be raped.*

- *Whenever anyone uses force to have sexual intercourse without the consent of the other party it is rape. 'Force' may include alcohol, weapons, intimidation, emotional blackmail, drugs or the victim's diminished mental capacity.*

- *Most women who have been beaten or abused by their husbands have also been raped by them. Being married doesn't give your partner license to force you to do anything against your will. Don't think women can't be raped by their husbands.*

- *Rape is one of the most under-reported crimes in the world - an average of only 16 per cent of all rapes are reported to the police.*

- *Everyone has the right to say 'no' or to change their mind. 'NO' means 'NO'.*

- *Rape doesn't only happen to women. Men and children are also victims of rape.*

- *Rape happens everywhere - at all times of the day and night. It can happen in the street, at work, in car parks, in hotel rooms, in public as well as remote places, but in fact almost 50 per cent of all rapes take place in the victim's home.*

- *Rape is rarely just a sexual crime. In many cases rape is accompanied by violent physical attack and the victims are brutally beaten because most rapists attack as a result of feelings of hate and aggression towards women. Also, realising the victim is the only witness, the rapist may decide to kill her to protect his identity.*

- *The number of reported rapes have trebled in recent years and yet the number of convicted rapists has stayed the same.*

- *The majority of rape victims are under 30 with many being less than 16-years-old.*

- *The majority of rapists tend to be lacking social and sexual confidence.*

- *Most rapes are planned well in advance. A small majority, however are opportunist attacks.*

- *Most rapists will use a weapon of some description. The most common is a knife.*

There are usually four categories of motivation:

1. Vindictive – the rape is used as a punishment.

2. Anger – the rape is a method of venting rage on somebody, anybody.

3. Sexual – to gratify some sexual desire, the rapists think they have the right to have sex with anyone they want.

4. Sadistic – the rapist's only aim is to gain sexual gratification by inflicting pain, extreme violence, mutilation or even death on their victim.

If you are threatened with rape, some do's and don'ts

DO
- *Remain calm.*
- *Try to deter the rapist by talking.*

- *Maintain eye contact.*
- *If necessary, yell and shout to draw attention to your situation.*
- *Try to bluff the attacker into thinking you are compliant.*
- *Run away as soon as the opportunity presents itself.*
- *Use anything at hand as a weapon.*
- *Study your attacker so you can give a good description of him.*
- *Remember which direction he left in.*
- *Note the way he operates - any conversation, anything unusual about his accent, terminology, etc.*
- *Report the crime to the police immediately.*

DON'T

- *Never cry or beg.*
- *Don't complain.*
- *Don't struggle half-heartedly. If you have to fight do it with all your might, fight to cripple and maim.*
- *Don't be submissive.*
- *Don't antagonise him with threats of reporting his actions to the authorities. Assure him you would be too ashamed and embarrassed to tell anyone.*
- *Don't stay around the crime scene.*
- *Do not wash, shower or change any of your clothes because you could be destroying vital evidence.*

STALKING

Over the last few years we have seen a much highlighted increase in the number of stalkers – someone who has become obsessed or infatuated with another person. The stalker becomes pathologically involved, following their victim around (and victim they certainly are) trying desperately to have a relationship of any kind with them. It is obvious if you are being stalked because the behaviour is so obsessive and inappropriate.

The overwhelming number of stalkers are men. Quite often they have been in a relationship with their female victims, or worse still, believe they have had a relationship even when they have not. A victim could be a mere acquaintance such as a neighbour, friend or work colleague. As many as one in four doctors, therapists and counsellors have become victims of stalking, some are known to have had several stalkers. Being stalked is not a compliment, because many frustrated stalkers are not content to simply follow their subject, all too often their actions result in verbal abuse, abusive letters, damage to property, physical assault and even murder. If you are being stalked, you are a victim of a crime. Do not ignore it. The stalker will not just 'go away'. These individuals are sick and in need of help, but don't be fooled into thinking you can help them. You must report a stalker to the police and keep on reporting it until action is taken.

Stalkers tend to fall into three main types: intimate, delusional and vengeful. They are all potentially dangerous.

Intimate

- *Over 50 per cent of all stalkers fall into this category.*
- *Although this can apply to women, they are usually men who can't accept that a relationship has ended. People often feel sorry for them, including the victim. This concern is generally unwarranted because studies have shown that these types of people were emotionally abusive and controlling during the relationship.*
- *Victims often unwittingly encourage the stalker by trying to 'let them down gently'. You should say 'No' only once to the stalker and then nothing else.*
- *You cannot reason with a stalker. For example 'I don't want a relationship now' is often interpreted as 'They'll want me back tomorrow' and 'It's not working out' as 'We can make things work if we try a bit harder'. The stalker believes that you could love them if you really tried.*
- *They can resort to emotional blackmail by threatening suicide.*

Delusional

- *Rarely have any contact with their victim.*
- *Schizophrenia or manic depression can result in delusional stalking.*
- *Delusional stalkers often come from emotionally deprived or abusive backgrounds.*
- *They may harbour a false belief that keeps them tied to their victims, such as 'if you knew me you'd love me'.*
- *Often the stalker actually believes that he is having a relationship with his victim, even though they may never have met.*
- *Some stalkers actually believe that their destiny is to spend the rest of their lives with their victim and are convinced, if they pursue them long enough, the victim will fall in love with them.*
- *Delusional stalkers are often unmarried, socially immature loners who are unable to establish close relationships. They rarely date and have had few, if any, sexual partners.*

- *Often they fantasize and pick victims who are unattainable such as pop stars, film stars, married people or even their doctor or priest.*

Vengeful

- *This type of stalker often has a vendetta against their victim because of an incident, real or imagined. Typical victims would be politicians or employers.*

- *Vengeful stalkers believe they are the victims.*

- *They stalk to try and 'get even' and often resort to violence.*

STALKER VIOLENCE

Many cases of stalking last for years but never become violent. However, don't assume you aren't in danger from a stalker as a significant number of cases have turned violent and become extremely dangerous very quickly. It is not only the victim themselves who are in danger because those around the victim may be perceived as a threat by the stalker and therefore must be removed. There are certain factors which may predict whether a stalker is likely to become violent:

- *Stalking more than one victim.*

- *Past criminal history not necessarily related to stalking.*

- *Alcohol or drug abuse.*

- *High degree, almost manic, obsession with their victim.*

- *Access to and knowledge of weapons.*

- *Huge amount of time spent stalking and prepared to travel long distances to be near their victim.*

If you are a stalking victim, some do's and don'ts

DO

- *Recognise that you are a victim of crime.*

- *Contact the police immediately.*

- *Increase your personal security.*

- *Tell the stalker 'No' but only once, then do not respond again. A response is what a stalker seeks.*

- *Keep a record of all incidences such as sightings, letters received, flowers and gifts, telephone calls and messages on your answering machine.*

- *Consider having a PO box for your mail and an ex-directory telephone number.*

- *Remove your name from any reserved parking spaces at the office.*

- *Destroy junk mail, don't just throw it in the dustbin.*

- *Get a mobile phone and keep it with you at all times - even by your bed.*

- *If you think you're being followed in the car, drive to the nearest police station. Never drive home or to a friend's house.*

DON'T

- *Never allow yourself to be alone with the stalker.*
- *Don't take the situation lightly or try to ignore it.*
- *Do not let the stalker take control of the situation.*
- *Don't respond to any of the stalker's requests or demands.*
- *Never directly confront the stalker.*
- *Don't invite a discussion or try to reason with them.*
- *Never discount any violent threats you may receive.*
- *Try not to feel intimidated - get help from the police, an employer or friend.*
- *Never give out your home address and telephone number.*
- *Don't accept packages unless you ordered them personally.*

FAMILY VIOLENCE

Family or domestic violence is sadly another vastly under-reported crime and it is a problem of epidemic proportions with often catastrophic consequences for the victims. The vast majority of victims are wives, although a surprising proportion of men are physically abused by their partners. After wives, the next largest group to suffer family violence and abuse are children. Although domestic violence usually occurs in the home, it can also happen in the homes of friends or family, in the workplace or even public places such as shops and car parks. More women are seriously injured by the men in their lives than in road accidents, rapes and muggings combined. Sufferers of domestic violence are more likely to be killed as a result than they are out on the streets.

Flight or fight is often not an option, particularly if there are children involved. Physical abuse or 'battering' is a repeated occurrence to establish dominance, power and control over another. It can become almost a ritual, recurring pattern of abuse that often ends up in rape as further punishment. If it has happened once it will happen again, and the relationship is not going to get better. Using their partner as a scapegoat for some incident that has happened somewhere else, such as problems at work, gambling losses, sexual jealousy are all very common reasons for violence in the home even if totally unjustified. Excessive alcohol will often trigger mindless lashing out with little or no provocation.

No-one deserves to be abused and no-one has the right to abuse another person. The first thing you need to do if you are suffering family violence is to admit it to yourself, then accept that it is not going to go away and seek professional help. Recognise and evaluate the warning signs of impending aggression and try to avoid those situations.

Be aware if your partner exhibits the following traits:

- *Overly possessive or jealous behaviour.*
- *Dictates what is your place in the home and insists on making all the decisions.*
- *Stops you spending time in the company of family and friends, especially those of the opposite sex.*
- *Controls all the finances, hides their income from you but insists that you divulge any income you may have.*
- *An inability to discuss feelings calmly and rationally.*
- *Extremely volatile, resorts to violence with or without the use of weapons. Can abuse family pets and destroys your property.*
- *Continuously criticises everything you do, say and wear.*
- *Mood swings with violent outbursts - verbal or physical.*

If you suffer family violence, some do's and don'ts

DO

- *You must accept that you are a victim in a potentially life-threatening situation.*
- *Make sure all family members are aware of emergency telephone numbers*
- *If your partner has hit you the chances are that they'll do it again. You must report it and get help.*
- *Collect evidence of any beatings such as photographs of any injuries, hospital reports, witnesses statements.*
- *You must try and escape; don't kid yourself things will get better because they won't.*

DON'T

- *Never stay with someone who beats you, especially for 'the sake of the children'.*
- *Don't wait for something terrible to happen before you call for help; you may leave it too late.*
- *Try not to antagonise your partner or exacerbate the situation; keep a low profile.*
- *Don't return the aggression; let the authorities handle it for you.*

HOME SECURITY

Not all acts of violence occur on the streets, many happen where you feel safest – in your own home. Around 95 per cent of all burglaries are opportunist crimes sparked off by obvious signs such as an open window, a flimsy door, a garden shed with tools on view, a ladder propped up in the back garden etc. By imagining you are a burglar you can assess the level of security at your home. Does the house look occupied? Is there anything obvious worth stealing? Is there a dog? Are there outside lights? Is the spare key hidden under a mat or plant pot? Your home is your castle so defend it!

Some do's and don'ts for home security

DO

- *Fit a 'peephole' so you can see who is outside before you open the door.*
- *Fit an outside light.*
- *Fit a chain.*
- *Have a panic button installed with your alarm.*
- *Keep a list of 'emergency' numbers by the phone because when you're under stress you probably won't be able to think straight.*
- *Ascertain what the caller wants before opening the door.*
- *If you're alone and you answer a knock at the door, give the impression of having company by calling out to your 'imaginary' guest.*
- *Always have your keys in your hand when you arrive home.*
- *Lock all accessible doors and windows at night.*
- *Close your curtains at night.*
- *If you do find yourself with intruders, lock yourself into a room - even pulling a chest of drawers across a door will deter most thieves.*
- *Arm yourself with anything nearby - never confront a burglar empty handed.*
- *Smash an upstairs window and scream out loud to scare the burglar(s) into making their escape.*
- *If you do see the burglar, mentally note his appearance and any distinguishing features.*
- *Arrange your furniture on the ground floor so there is no direct line from the window to the*

door. *Anything you can do that will slow a burglar down gives you more time to respond and for the police to arrive.*

DON'T

- *Never let a stranger into your home when you're alone. If you need a workman to come round to repair something, arrange to have a friend or neighbour with you.*

- *Do not keep large amounts of cash in your house.*

- *Never judge by appearances - children and people in uniform may be a ploy to gain entry into your house.*

- *Don't worry about keeping the caller waiting while you check their credentials, genuine repairmen won't mind. Never believe they are genuine just because they carry a pass, anyone can fake an ID card.*

- *Don't advertise the fact that you live alone by putting your name on the door plate or in the telephone directory.*

- *Never put an address on your house keys and never leave spare keys in an obvious place like under the mat or behind a plant pot.*

- *If you think that someone is trying to break in don't go and investigate, call the police.*

- *Don't try to stop the burglar taking your possessions. Don't even consider confronting the burglar. You won't even know who or what you are facing but if you do encounter him don't try to block his exit.*

- *Take care not to get yourself cornered with your escape route blocked.*

- *Don't touch anything until the police arrive.*

- *If you have a dog, don't keep it locked in one room at night. Allow it to roam freely and try to persuade it to sleep at the top of the stairs.*

Nuisance telephone callers

There are people who use the telephone as a tool for intimidation and who get a thrill from making malicious or obscene calls. Such calls can cause immense anxiety and distress, and are a direct invasion of someone's home.

- *Never answer the phone by saying your name or number.*

- *A caller who hangs up without actually speaking may be trying to ascertain if your house is occupied.*

- *Beware of people who telephone you to find out information about you, your family, your work colleagues or your neighbours. Although the call may be genuine you should always treat them with suspicion.*

- *Seriously consider having an answer machine or using a professional answering service, but never give specific details about your whereabouts on your message. If you are a female living alone, get a male friend to record your answer-phone message.*

- *Report frequent nuisance or obscene telephone calls to your telephone company.*

- *If you receive a nuisance call and the caller doesn't speak, don't try to coax them into talking – just replace the handset.*

- *Stay calm because it might just be a genuine wrong number or a friend playing a joke.*

- *Don't start chastising the caller, telling them they're sick or depraved. They want to generate a reaction from you and you will be playing into their hands.*

- *If the caller persists and you are unable to ignore the ringing of the phone, blow a shrill whistle down the receiver, but don't speak.*

- *Try not to get drawn into a ridiculous and degenerative conversation.*

- *You can unplug the phone which means that the caller hears the ringing tone but you don't have to put up with incessant calls.*

- *Never leave the phone 'off the hook' which can cause problems at the telephone exchange.*

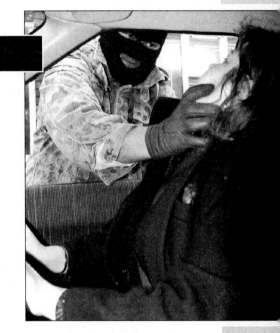

VEHICLE SECURITY

There are obvious things you can do like taking care not to leave your keys in the ignition, keeping the doors locked, investing in an alarm system and parking in a safe location. You may think that you're safer when travelling in a vehicle because it is moving and to a certain extent this is true. However, if you break down, you may find yourself in a more vulnerable situation, especially if you are alone in a remote location and it's night. Most modern cars are relatively reliable, but you need to ensure that you keep it maintained to minimise the risk of breaking down.

Some do's and don'ts for car security

DO
- *Make sure your car is in good running order and regularly check the oil, the tyres, the windscreen wipers, etc.*

- *Make sure all the doors and windows are in good working order, that they close properly, lock and so on.*

- *Always lock your doors whenever you are in the car.*

- *Always carry a first aid pack in your car.*

- *When walking up to your vehicle make sure you have your car keys ready in your hand.*

- *Always park in well-lit, busy, open areas, preferably where there is an attendant or security staff nearby.*

- *Always reverse into your parking space and so, if you have to make a quick getaway, you can drive straight out and won't find yourself trying to reverse out of a tight spot.*

- *Be wary of anyone trying to attract your attention at petrol stations, etc. Thieves and car-jackers often use this method to distract you away from your car.*

- *Before getting into your car make a quick check around it and look inside before unlocking it.*

- *If you find your car has been broken into, always check there is no-one hiding underneath or in the back of the vehicle.*

- *Sound your horn loudly to attract attention to yourself.*

- *If someone tries to get into your car while you're driving, for example, as you stop at a red light, you may have several improvised weapons within reach. A torch or can of de-icer can act as a good deterrent, but remember that whatever you use as a weapon you may have to justify to the police later.*

DON'T

- *Never leave items of value on display in your vehicle.*

- *Never leave items in your vehicle which indicate your sex such as a lady's umbrella, articles of clothing or perfume.*

- *Never leave your handbag or briefcase on the front passenger seat where they can be easily grabbed. Keep them in the front footwell and loop the strap over the gear stick if possible.*

- *If you need to have the window down, make sure it's not wide enough for anyone to get their hand inside.*

- *Don't be tempted to park in an unauthorised area because if you return to find your car has been clamped you will be very vulnerable, especially if it's at night.*

- *Don't keep your driving documents in the glove compartment.*

- *Don't keep your car keys on the same key ring as your house keys.*

- *In the cold weather never leave your car running to warm up while you go back in the house - stay in your car.*

- *Never leave babies and young children alone in the car, even for just a few minutes.*

- *Try to avoid renting a car which is obviously rented because tourists are an obvious target.*

- *If you see a group of youths hanging around your car don't approach them, get help.*

- *If you break down, never accept unsolicited offers of assistance, wait for the emergency services.*

- *Never give lifts to strangers or people you don't know well.*

- *If someone tries to flag you down, particularly if it's at night, don't stop under any circumstances. Drive on to a safe place and call for help.*

- *If you think you're being followed never drive home, drive to a safe haven such as a police station, petrol station or late-night supermarket.*

ROAD RAGE

Road rage may not be new but it does seem to be on the increase. Try to avoid a confrontation by taking care to drive at a safe speed, give clear indications in plenty of time, stay in the correct lane on the motorway, avoid being deliberately obstructive, let people in from side roads and don't cut up other drivers.

- *If you find yourself being aggressively hassled by another driver, smile and apologise by mouthing 'sorry' if you made a mistake. This will usually appease most drivers.*

- *If they overtake you aggressively, slow down to put some distance between you and them.*

- *If the other driver draws alongside, avoid direct eye contact.*

- *Never make obscene hand gestures.*

- *Avoid being forced to stop if at all possible.*

- *Make sure all your doors and windows are locked.*

- *stay calm and remain in your vehicle at all times unless you are involved in an accident when you should still try to remain calm and cool.*

- *If someone tries to get into your car and you aren't able to drive away, sound your horn to draw attention to yourself.*

TRAVEL SECURITY

Tourism is a huge business with far-flung, exotic corners of the world becoming easier to get to. International business travel is continuously growing and business executives can frequently find themselves visiting countries where the culture, time zones and language are completely unfamiliar to them. However, whether you are one mile or 10,000 miles from home the same safety rules still apply. When you are away the three things you should consider are: Have I left my home safe? Are my personal belongings, property and baggage safe? Am I safe?

Some travel safety do's and don'ts

DO

- *The way you dress is just as important as the way you project yourself. Dress down to avoid drawing attention to yourself and to minimise the risk of your clothes hampering your escape should you need to run away from trouble.*

- *On the subway or on escalators keep your bag near to the wall, away from the people running past you.*

- *Consider carrying a 'dummy' giveaway wallet or purse with a few out-of-date credit cards and a small amount of money. Keep it in the place where you would normally carry it such as* in your inside jacket pocket or handbag and conceal your actual wallet or purse somewhere else.

- If you are unfamiliar with the area take a licensed taxi, for example a black cab in London or a yellow cab in New York. Don't walk if you don't know the neighbourhood. If you have no choice but to use a minicab try to do some preliminary checks if possible and always try to travel in company.

- Try to stay in the light near to other people when travelling on public transport, particularly at stations.

- On a bus chose a seat where you can see ahead to your stop clearly. If you're unhappy about other people getting off at the same stop, stay on until the next stop or if necessary the bus station and get a taxi back to your destination.

- Take particular care on the road to and from the airport, especially when abroad - most robberies take place on these roads.

- Be aware that in some foreign countries bandits will dress as police or security officials to rob tourists.

- When travelling abroad remember that you may be a tourist but you are still a guest in that country and you should show respect for its culture. For example, in a Muslim country, such as Tunisia or Morocco. women should be careful where they show their arms and legs, because this is considered disrespectful and can be taken as an insult.

- Try to research the country you are thinking about visiting before you go.

- Get as much information as you can about local car hire, taxis, hotels, local customs and places to avoid.

- Learn a few phrases in the local language so you can ask for help if necessary.

- Be polite but firm if approached by a prostitute and make it clear that you're not interested. If she is accompanied by a man he is most likely her pimp.

- Always travel as lightly as possible so you can move quickly if necessary, plus you will be able to use your hands for self-defence.

- Always make sure you have a map of your destination. A good city map will show suitable 'safe havens' such as hospitals, police stations and public buildings. Try to remember obvious 'markers' along your route, that way if you take a taxi you will at least know if you're travelling in the right direction.

- Plan where you will leave your car and don't make on-the-spot decisions. Always park in official car parks.

- If family or friends take you to the airport to see you off, make sure you say your goodbyes before you get to the airport. Groups of people kissing and hugging are an obvious target for opportunist criminals and they will steal your bags in a moment while you're distracted with your farewells.

- The most dangerous part of an airport is landside, so once you've checked in go through customs as quickly as you can so you are airside. You will be much safer here as everyone has gone through security checks. It is the same when you reach your destination. While you are collecting your baggage you are relatively secure, but once you go through customs you are landside again and must heighten your awareness.

- *At the airport you have all your luggage and all your valuables on you and criminals know that. Keep everything as close to you as you can and remain alert to those around you. Once you get to your hotel place your valuables in the hotel safe immediately.*

- *Never put your valuables in your hold luggage; keep them with you on the plane.*

- *Once you've collected your baggage at your destination distribute your valuables amongst your heavy luggage and make sure the cases lock.*

- *If possible travel in a group.*

- *Try to get away from the airport as quickly as you can.*

- *If you are hiring a car and pick it up at the airport, be on your guard! Any criminal watching an individual or family going to the car compound on the airport bus will know that they are carrying a lot of money.*

- *If you rent a car abroad try to choose something popular and available locally and steer clear of anything flashy which stands out and makes you an obvious target.*

- *Check that any hire vehicle is in good repair.*

- *If possible, opt for air-conditioning in a hire car in order to avoid opening the windows.*

- *As you leave the compound be at your most alert - many criminals are waiting outside just watching for you to make a mistake and get out of your car. Follow all the security precautions in your car previously mentioned, like locking your doors, keeping your windows closed, etc.*

- *Make a note of local emergency numbers.*

- *Only carry one reputable credit card with you and leave the rest safely locked in the safe at the hotel.*

- *Keep your hotel key with you at all times.*

- *Put your valuables in the hotel safe - cash, passport, credit cards, etc.*

- *Keep your hotel door locked at all times, and make sure you know the identity of any callers before opening the door.*

- *Read the fire instructions and make sure you know where the nearest exit is.*

- *Put the 'Do not disturb' sign on the door, even when you're out, to give the impression that the room is occupied.*

- *Leave the light or television on when you go out of the room.*

- *Vary the time that you leave and return to your hotel and don't always take the same route.*

- *Be aware when entering public conveniences.*

- *Be alert to scams such as a stranger spilling a drink on you, which could be a diversion for an accomplice.*

- *Be aware of pickpockets. Remember, they don't work in quiet streets but operate swiftly and discreetly in crowds.*

DON'T

- *Don't wear your valuable diamond jewellery or your expensive Rolex watch.*

- *Try not to use trains at night. If it's unavoidable, don't pick unmanned stations and don't wait on the platform.*

- *Don't sit alone on the train. Try to sit near to a group of people. If you're worried about the look of someone at your station, don't get off - wait until the next station.*

- *On a bus don't travel on the upper deck, stay downstairs close to the driver.*

- *Don't go to a country with a very high crime rate, as a tourist you are a prime target. Be aware of what the actual risks are.*

- *On the plane by all means have a drink but don't have too many! You want to arrive at your destination with your wits about you.*

- *Don't carry luggage for anyone else under any circumstances.*

- *Never discuss your travel plans with anyone.*

- *Never take a vehicle which isn't clearly marked as a taxi and check the driver's face with his identification card.*

- *Don't jump into a hire car and drive straight off. It's only sensible to spend a short while familiarising yourself with the car and making certain you know exactly where you're going and how to get out of the airport complex.*

- *Don't flash large amounts of cash around.*

- *Never let friendly ambience and a couple of drinks cloud your judgement and common sense.*

- *Never leave a stranger to watch your bags on the beach or around the pool, this is a popular ploy with thieves.*

- *When you need to change money make sure you go into a bank and don't use one of the little booths on the street. It may appear that you'll get a better rate on the street but you could end up with a black eye and no wallet!*

- *Don't buy trinkets from street vendors.*

- *Don't carry any valuables in obvious places.*

HIJACK

Although the possibility of you becoming a hostage victim is slim, it is still a possibility. Terrorists are known to have little or no regard for human life. If you are innocently caught up in a hijack situation, you must stay as calm as possible and try to think clearly and concisely.

Some do's and don'ts if you are caught in a hijack

DO

- *Hide any documents which could single you out or increase hostility towards you.*

- *Co-operate with the terrorists - prepare meals, tend the injured or sick, look after the terrorists themselves.*

- *Avoid eye contact with the terrorists.*

- *Reassure fellow hostages. Make allowances for behaviour caused by stress.*

- *Drink plenty of water.*

- *Be prepared for difficulties with sanitation.*

- *If you manage to build up a rapport with the terrorists, try to get improved conditions for everyone.*

- *Keep your mind occupied.*

- *Talk to the kidnappers about personal matters - show them pictures of your children - try to get them to see you as an individual not as a victim. If they begin to identify with you personally, it will be more difficult for them to hurt you.*

- *If a rescue attempt is made, get on the floor and protect your head with your arms. Do not move until you are told it is safe to do so.*

DON'T

- *Don't be aggressive.*

- *Don't draw attention to yourself because you could run the risk of being singled out.*

- *Don't drink alcohol.*

- *Do not try to dissuade the terrorists from their political cause - it could be safer to agree with them.*

- *Don't try to be a hero if a rescue attempt is made. Follow instructions to leave the vehicle, aircraft or building quickly because it may have been wired with explosives.*

KIDNAP

In 1999 kidnap for a ransom reached a record high across the world. Of 1,789 known kidnappings 92 per cent occurred in only 10 countries, with Latin America accounting for 70 per cent of the total. However, as with rape, the actual number of kidnappings is likely to be much higher as many go unreported and are dealt with privately. When a British national is kidnapped abroad the Foreign Office always insists that the government of the country concerned take no action which could harm the hostage. British policy is never to give in to ransom demands.

Do's and don'ts if you are a kidnap victim

DO

- *Be aware that businessmen and women are most at risk, but celebrities such as footballers are also targets of kidnap gangs.*

- *If you feel your line of work puts you in danger, take out kidnap insurance.*

- *If you think you may be at risk, take stringent and comprehensive security measures.*

- *If you are kidnapped, avoid struggling but try to attract attention to yourself - witnesses may be able to give police valuable information.*

- *Stay calm.*

- *Try to work out where you're being taken - look for landmarks. If you are blindfolded or in a vehicle with no windows listen for sounds which might give you tell-tale signs of where you are.*

- *Try to work out your route by the movement of the vehicle.*

- *Remember, kidnappers can keep their victims in anything from windowless, darkened cells to almost normal living conditions.*

- *Try to get to know your kidnappers so you can assess how you should behave. Be co-operative.*

- *If you don't have any reading material you must try to keep your mind active - recite songs and poems, work out sums and puzzles, invent stories, etc.*

- *If you find yourself bound and gagged try to follow these brief guidelines:-*

- *Relax as you are tied to a chair and slump with the small of your back away from the back of the chair, that way when you straighten up there may be enough slack for you to escape.*

- *Keep your chest expanded until your kidnappers have finished tying your bonds.*

- *Try to keep knees and ankles apart.*

- *Try to keep your hands slightly apart too.*

- *If you are gagged try to catch the gag in your teeth to prevent it being forced all the way back in your mouth.*

- *If blindfolded try to rub it up against a shoulder or wall, but don't push it down because your nose will get in the way.*

- *If you are with other people, rely on teamwork.*

- *If you are asked to pay a ransom for someone else always inform the police but keep it away from the press. Payment will not necessarily result in the release of the hostage and the kidnappers may demand more.*

- *Get as much information from the kidnappers as possible and keep any written communications clean for forensic teams.*

DON'T

- *Don't become aggressive. Remember that you're only valuable as a hostage when you are alive.*

- *Don't attempt to escape unless you are certain of your plan's success. If you're not certain of where you are it may be safer to stay put, especially if they are not mistreating you.*

CAUGHT IN A CROWD

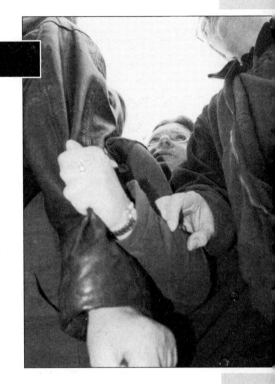

A crowd that is angry or panicking can be extremely frightening and dangerous and your biggest danger is falling to the ground and being trampled on, or being crushed as the crowd presses forward. You may be part of a crowd voluntarily, at a sports stadium, for example, or at a rally or demonstration when the mood of the crowd changes for some reason.

Some do's and don'ts if you're caught in a crowd

DO

- *Avoid crowds where you know there could be risk of unrest, such as volatile sporting events or political demonstrations.*
- *When you arrive at a large event or venue make sure you check out the safest and quickest exit routes.*
- *Always stay away from the centre of the crowd.*
- *Try to stay calm.*
- *Take steps to edge your way out of the crowd.*
- *Try to stay on your feet at all times.*
- *Fold your arms in front of you, in that way you may be able to create a bit of breathing space around you.*
- *If you fall or are knocked to the ground, curl yourself into a ball with your hands around your head. Try to crawl to the nearest immovable object such as a wall or a tree - somewhere where the crowd will be forced to separate and where you will have your biggest chance of getting back on your feet.*

DON'T

- *If you get inadvertently caught up in a marauding crowd, don't panic.*
- *Never stand at the front of a crowd, by a stage or barrier because you are most likely to be crushed there.*
- *Try not to be pushed against walls, pillars or steps, etc.*
- *Try not to leave a venue with the main crowd, especially if 'rival' spectators are leaving at the same time. Leave a little early or wait until most of the crowd has left.*

DEFENCE AGAINST DOGS

An attack by a dog, no matter how small, can be a terrifying experience, not least because you have no way of reasoning with the animal. With a dog bite, in fact with any bite human or animal, you should always seek medical attention because there is a very real risk of infection. Be aware of rabies; although it can be spread by many animals, you are still most at risk from dogs. A single bite or even a lick from an infected animal can pass the disease on to a human. If left untreated, rabies is a fatal disease and if you are bitten by a dog in a high-risk country, wash the wound carefully and get medical help immediately.

Dogs often try to bite and lock on to a part of the body, normally a limb. If you have time take your coat off and use it to pad one arm then offer this protected limb to the dog and push your arm as far back into the dogs throat as you can. Once the dog has locked on, strike it hard on the head or nose or go for the eyes. Keep on striking until the animal is incapacitated or even dead otherwise it will just become more aggressive. If you end up on the ground, roll into a tight ball and play dead. Keep your hands over your ears, face, throat and neck. Don't scream or thrash about. If you are on your back with a large dog on top of you, try to hold its head away from your face, throw your legs around the dog's body and squeeze hard in a scissor action. Roll over, grab the dog's front legs and force them apart with a snapping action. An attacking dog will always try to paw down any barriers in its way and so a stick, broom, briefcase, etc. will help to bar its path. The dog will always attack the object before you.

If you are out jogging and a dog charges at you, stop! Try dropping or throwing something like a bag or hat to tempt the dog to stop and investigate. Sometimes with small dogs a swift kick may do the trick; you may even be able to pick up a small dog by the scruff of its neck and remove it. However, with a large powerful dog you only have two choices: Be submissive and play dead, hoping the animal will give up and go away; or, if you fear you are going to be mauled, you must break the dog's spirit or kill it. You will be bitten, but you will stay alive and you were going to be bitten anyway!

Of the two choices, naturally the first is always the most preferable.

Some do's and don'ts when faced with an aggressive dog

DO

- *Stand still.*

- *Let the dog sniff you.*

- *Stay calm.*

- *Say 'no' in a low, commanding tone of voice.*

- *Try 'good boy' etc in a gentle, non-aggressive voice.*

- *Protect your face and groin.*

- *Roll into a ball and play dead.*

- *Let the dog be the boss.*

DON'T

- *Never run away.*

- *Don't scream and shout.*

- *Don't stare into the dog's eyes, in fact avoid all eye contact because this is a challenge to the dog.*

- *Don't move until the dog has gone, but if you have to move, back away slowly.*

- *Never fight unless you fear for your life.*

- *Don't grab it by the tail.*

- *Never hesitate to kill the animal.*

OTHER ANIMALS

Snakes

Simple rule: if you come across a snake, leave it alone, back away slowly and don't prod it or touch it at all. If you are bitten by a snake, always assume that it is venomous. Even non-venomous snakes can cause infection. Wash the bite with soap and water as soon as you can and get medical attention. Any snake-bite should be considered a medical emergency. Try to immobilise the area that has been bitten and keep it lower than the heart if possible. Wrap something as tightly as you can 2"-4" above the bite, but do not cut off the blood flow completely. Do not make any incisions on or around the wound and do not attempt to suck out any venom.

Bulls

Bulls will usually leave you alone unless you antagonise them in some way. Running away from a charging bull is not going to help unless there is a fence or wall you can get behind. A bull will easily out-run you. If you cannot get to safety, remain still and, as the bull approaches you, throw something – your hat, coat, etc. away from you. The bull should veer towards the object you have thrown. When the bull's attention has been distracted, try and move away slowly, but do not run and do not lie down, a bull will trample you.

I believe most, if not all confrontations are won with your brain and not your brawn. My **REACT** system makes you use your brain before your fists. Any fool can punch someone in the mouth, but it takes understanding and insight to stop a situation getting out of hand. Recognise, evaluate, select an alternative, concentrate then terminate. Simple! All you have to do now is make **REACT** part of your daily life. But remember, if you ever do have to defend yourself physically, and I hope and pray you never do, keep this one thought in mind – in a real fight everybody loses something, even if it's only a little pride or dignity. **REACT** will help you to survive and now that you have read the book I hope you will walk with more confidence and refuse to ever be a victim!

I only have one more thing to say..... read it again!

Stay safe

Steve Collins